Victorian Masters of Mystery

No. III.]　　　　JUNE, 1870.　　　　[Price One Shilling.

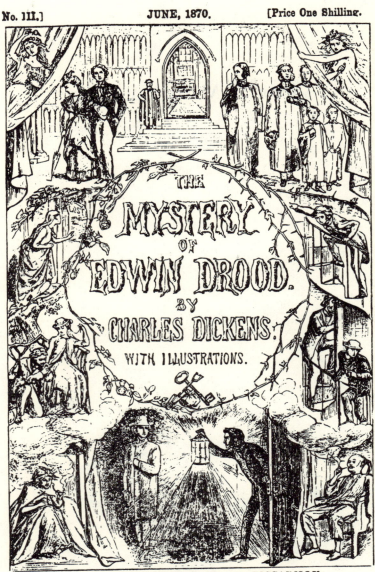

THE
MYSTERY
OF
EDWIN DROOD.
BY
CHARLES DICKENS.
WITH ILLUSTRATIONS.

LONDON: CHAPMAN & HALL, 193, PICCADILLY.

Advertisements to be sent to the Publishers, and ADAMS & FRANCIS, 59, Fleet Street, E.C.
[*The right of Translation is reserved.*]

A cover design for one of the most
famous Victorian mysteries

VICTORIAN MASTERS OF MYSTERY

From Wilkie Collins to Conan Doyle

Audrey Peterson

FREDERICK UNGAR PUBLISHING CO.
New York

ACKNOWLEDGMENTS

I should like to express my appreciation for the courtesy and assistance extended to me by the staff of the London Library, St. James's Square, London, and by the staff of the Special Collections in the University Research Library at the University of California at Los Angeles.

Library of Congress Cataloging in Publication Data

Peterson, Audrey.
    Victorian masters of mystery.

    Bibliography: p.
    Includes index.
    1. Detective and mystery stories, English—History and criticism.   2. English fiction—19th century—History and criticism.   3. Collins, Wilkie, 1824–1889—Criticism and interpretation.   4. Dickens, Charles, 1812–1870. Mystery of Edwin Drood.   5. Le Fanu, Joseph Sheridan, 1814–1873—Criticism and interpretation.   6. Doyle, Arthur Conan, Sir, 1859–1930—Characters—Sherlock Holmes.   I. Title.
PR878.D4P4   1983   823'.0872'09   83-19858
    ISBN 0-8044-2697-X
    ISBN 0-8044-6651-3 (pbk.)

For Laura

Contents

1

Beginnings: The London Constabulary

When Edgar Allan Poe published his famous tales of crime and murder in the 1840s, he created a new form in fiction, for which he has been justly acclaimed the father of the mystery story. This paternity did not, however, produce immediate offspring. Perhaps because Poe was less widely read in his own day than his genius deserved, it was not until the 1890s that his brilliant detective, Auguste Dupin, found a worthy successor in Sir Arthur Conan Doyle's Sherlock Holmes.

What happened in mystery fiction between Poe and Conan Doyle? Surprisingly little occurred in America until later in the century; it was in Great Britain that the genre developed, not following the direction laid down by Poe, as one might expect, but emerging instead from the social novel. Victorian novelists, primarily concerned with giving lively portrayals of society and its foibles, moved almost incidentally into works that anticipate the flourishing detection and suspense industry of the twentieth century. Given the general interest in crime and its effects upon society, it was inevitable that methods of policing and detection of crime would become popular topics. Equally, the moral implications of personal crimes, those committed from passion or greed, had a universal appeal. The growth of literacy throughout the nineteenth century created a new popular audience eager for excitement, and writers were quick to respond to this lucrative market. The label "sensation novelists" came to be applied to writers like Charles Dickens, Wilkie Collins, and Sheridan Le Fanu, who liberally laced their works with grisly scenes of crime and murder.

The figure of the detective, which has become central to so much of twentieth-century mystery fiction, first began to appear in this period, though not always in a favorable light. The highly respected Scotland Yard detectives of modern fiction—Ngaio Marsh's Roderick Alleyn, Michael Innes's John Appleby, Josephine Tey's Alan Grant, and P. D. James's Adam Dalgliesh, to name a few—are the products of a long struggle to establish a reliable police system in England.

Public acceptance of such a system was necessary before mystery and detective fiction as we know it today could have its beginnings. As Dorothy Sayers once observed, "the detective-story could not flourish until public sympathy had veered round to the side of law and order. . . . The tendency in early crime literature is to admire the cunning and astuteness of the criminal."[1] Once the balance shifted to admiration of those who detect crime rather than of those who commit it, the time was ripe for the rogue hero to give way to the protector of society.

As late as the middle of the eighteenth century, there was no official police force in the British Isles.[2] Each local parish had a justice of the peace who served as magistrate, an unpaid position that rotated among citizens as a public service. Each justice had a constable to assist him, and since persons appointed as constable could hire substitutes, this function was often performed by elderly or incompetent persons. The practice of paying spies and informers to bring evidence against criminals was widespread. While this concept of "setting a thief to catch a thief" had its practical value, it was obviously subject to corruption. Bounty hunters could manufacture evidence or inform against innocent persons in order to obtain rewards, with the result that in the public mind those who detected and reported criminals were often as much abhorred as the culprits themselves. Before public support could be obtained for an official police system, the public image of law enforcement had to change.

A major step in this transformation was taken by Henry Fielding, who contributed to posterity not only his great novels but also the beginnings of a reliable system of dealing with crime. When he became magistrate of the Bow Street court in London's Covent Garden in 1747, he dispensed with many of the payoffs and other corrupt practices that had been rife, gathered together a small corps of constables for whom he obtained a modest pay, and through sheer force of will injected some order and honesty into the workings of the court. After his death in

1754 his work was carried on by his brother John, who managed to get some regular pay for a force of foot and horse patrols and for a small group of investigating officers who became known as the Bow Street Runners. Admired for their daring and resourcefulness, these first English detective officers became subjects of popular myth, making dramatic arrests of murderers and gaining favorable publicity through their service to aristocratic patrons.

But, ironically, the principles of honesty and integrity established by the Fieldings did not always prevail. The Runners' basic pay was small, most of their income being derived from rewards and gifts from patrons. They were permitted to work for private citizens outside their official duties and often received generous sums in return for solving cases successfully. Some fell from grace and became involved in scandals, sharing loot with the criminals they were sent to arrest or setting up innocent victims in order to collect rewards, as their predecessors had done.[3] Nevertheless, such cases were in the minority, and the Runners did much on the whole to improve the public image of law officers.

A novel entitled *Richmond: Scenes in the Life of a Bow Street Runner*, which appeared in 1827, gives a lively example of the change taking place in the popular view of crime detection. The "rogue hero" had been a staple of English fiction in the eighteenth century, from the works of Daniel Defoe to Henry Fielding's own *Jonathan Wild* (1743), and continued to appear well into the nineteenth century in such works as Harrison Ainsworth's *Jack Sheppard* (1839). What *Richmond* depicts is the transformation of the rogue hero—whose typical progress was from rags to riches to the gallows—into a reformed character who becomes an admirable officer of the law.

Published anonymously, *Richmond* purports to be a "memoir" but is undoubtedly fiction.[4] The story begins in pure picaresque tradition with likable young Tom Richmond as the rogue hero who breaks away from home and takes to the road. After engaging in a series of escapades and living for some time with a band of gypsies, Tom becomes "sick of the uncertainty of a precarious livelihood"[5] but realizes that his restless nature makes him unsuited for the usual kinds of steady employment. When he meets an old aquaintance who is now a Bow Street Runner, Tom joins the force and discovers his ideal vocation. Aided by his former knowledge of the criminal world, he enjoys plenty of adventure while remaining on the right side of the law. He marries his mistress and adopts the middle-class virtues against which he had originally rebelled.

Richmond shows the Bow Street Runners as a group of bold men thoroughly dedicated to their calling. In the series of cases Tom recounts, he displays a rough code of honor that has much in common with the private eyes of the hard-boiled school of detective fiction of the 1930s. Like Dashiell Hammett's Continental Op, Tom idealizes "good" women. Restoring a kidnapped child to the beautiful and grieving mother, he accepts her purse of gold but would have been satisfied with no reward other than the knowledge of her happiness. Like Raymond Chandler's Philip Marlowe, he deplores the degenerate behavior of the idle rich: breaking up the fashionable ring of forgers and gamblers who had defrauded a young heir to an estate, Richmond condemns the false standards of "this profligate age."[6] Whether or not his idealized picture of the Runners was altogether true, it nevertheless reflected a strong element of public admiration that had never been accorded to the spies and thief-takers of an earlier age.

Another memoir of an adventurer-turned-policeman appeared at about the same as *Richmond* and had an even greater impact on public opinion. This was the real life story of François Eugène Vidocq, who began his adult life as a fugitive and became the first chief of the Sûreté, the detective division of the French police, formed in 1812. Soon after his retirement in 1827, Vidocq published his *Memoirs* in Paris, translations of which promptly appeared in England, where they were enormously popular at the very time that the Prime Minister, Sir Robert Peel, was trying to get a bill through parliament to establish an English police system.

While Vidocq's *Memoirs*, which were probably ghost-written,[7] contain many racy and highly fictionalized episodes, they give a dramatic picture of his actual transformation from convict to police chief. Imprisoned in his youth for deserting from the army, Vidocq was convicted of aiding other prisoners to escape, an accusation he always denied. He himself, however, became famous for his escapes from galleys and prisons,[8] recounting in the *Memoirs* an incredible series of adventures among the criminal classes. Despite the gusto with which these episodes are recalled, Vidocq injects a moral theme into his narrative that becomes more insistent with time: after each escape he tries to go straight, engaging in legitimate occupations from which he is repeatedly driven through betrayal by former criminal associates. Like Richmond's, his desire to lead a life of respectability leads him to offer his services to the police as an informer.[9]

The spectacular career that had made him a legend among the criminal element now served him well in his new role, and he eventually received the pardon he sought. As a detective, Vidocq became a legendary figure, with his flamboyance, his genius at disguises, and his implacable dedication to tracking down the culprit. His *Memoirs* inspired in France such fictional detectives as Balzac's Vautrin and Gaboriau's Lecoq, influenced Poe in America, and helped to sway public opinion in Great Britain on the police-force issue.

France had established a centralized police force long before such a concept was accepted in England. The British were deeply averse to forming a government-controlled police that might become an instrument of political repression. The French system was regarded with mixed feelings. The very word "gendarme" sounded alarmingly military, and the French police did indeed engage at times in political espionage that threatened individual liberty. At the same time, the growth of crime, especially in the cities, made the competence of the French system attractive. The English began to see the hopeless inefficiency of the local parish system, under which the perpetrator of a crime could not be pursued over the border into the next parish. A unique feature in the success of the Bow Street

Runners had been their permission to travel throughout the British Isles and even sometimes abroad in pursuit of a thief or murderer. Bills proposing a professional police force had been repeatedly introduced into Parliament and defeated in the years before 1829; in that year the first major step was taken with the passage of Peel's Metropolitan Police Act.

With Peel's "Bobbies" patrolling the streets of London, people gradually began to look with some favor upon the professional police force. The administrators of the new system maintained what today would be called a low profile, wisely stressing the prevention of crime and eliminating much of the practice of large rewards that had led to corruption in the past. When detective services were needed, they were at first performed by officers of the regular force, either in uniform or in plain clothes. The Bow Street Runners still continued to function until 1839, when they were officially disbanded.

Still aware of the tendency of some segments of the public to regard those who pursued criminals as spies, the commissioners waited until 1842 to establish an official detective branch. Known as the Detective Department, this first group of eight plainclothes officers was the forerunner of the renowned Criminal Investigation Department of Scotland Yard. In method and manner the first officers were much like the Bow Street Runners—indeed, some of them were former Runners themselves—but unlike that group, the Detective Department acquired a reputation for honesty, remaining free for many years from scandal and corruption.

By mid-century, admirable pictures of the police detective began to appear, both in fiction and in the press. In 1849 a series of stories entitled "Recollections of a Detective Police-Officer" appeared in *Chambers's Edinburgh Journal*, spawning a series of detective casebooks which became a popular form from the 1850s onwards. Under the name "Waters," a pseudonym for a journalist named William Russell,[10] the "Recollections" recount a series of cases handled by a gentlemanly officer who lost his fortune through youthful folly and has joined the Metropolitan Police in order to earn a livelihood for himself and his wife. While the events purport to have occurred in the 1830s, they are clearly based on the new Detective Department. The character of Waters is dramatically different from that of reformed scoundrels like Richmond or Vidocq. Gone are the racy episodes and the flamboyant derring-do; the emphasis now is on the detective as a model of middle-class respectability. With his refinement of speech and manner, Waters could step out of the pages of a popular Victorian romance. In the execution of his duty, he seeks not merely to gain evidence against a suspect but to arrive at the truth. "My duty," he declares, "was quite as much the vindication of innocence as the detection of guilt."[11] In some of his cases he becomes a knight-errant to ladies in distress and often gives support to the happy outcome of romantic episodes. Collected in book form in 1856, the "Recollections" reached a wide audience, including those who were reassured by the preface that "not one line can raise a blush to the most sensitive cheek."[12]

Such fictional accounts as the *Recollections* provided welcome support to the fledgling Detective Department. The press had also begun to take favorable notice of their activities, notably in the laudatory newspaper accounts in 1849 of the officers who had captured the notorious murderers, Frederick and Maria Manning. Even more significant was the praise given to the officers in a series of articles by Charles Dickens in his magazine *Household Words* beginning in 1850, as shall be seen in more detail in Chapter 3. As the most popular novelist of the day, Dickens exerted a powerful influence over public opinion, and no history of the British police is complete without its reference to the encouragement derived from Dickens's glowing accounts of the officers of the London Detective Department.

Crime and detection were popular topics in the nineteenth century in the subliterary pulp fiction—the "shilling shockers" and "penny-a-liners"—addressed to the titillation of the lowest class of readers. While the existence of such works adds to an awareness of popular taste, the present volume is primarily concerned with looking at works of genuine literary merit. Chapter 2 examines the work of Wilkie Collins, who was the first to apply the mystery formula to the full-length novel. Chapter 3 discusses the contributions of Charles Dickens to detective literature and to the mystery format. Chapter 4 deals with Sheridan Le Fanu, the master of horror and suspense. Chapter 5 gives a sampling of minor writers whose work appeared between 1860 and 1890. The closing chapter presents a brief overview of the great master of detective fiction, Arthur Conan Doyle.

2

Wilkie Collins and the Mystery Novel

Wilkie Collins's friend, the novelist Charles Reade, once said, "For literary ingenuity in building up a plot and investing it with mystery, give me good old Wilkie Collins against the world."[1] It was this talent for artfully constructed plots of suspense that earned for Collins the title of father of English mystery fiction. But Collins did not set out to be a mystery writer. Like his contemporaries Dickens and Thackeray, he wrote social novels that appealed to a wide popular audience. Of his twenty-five or so novels and dozens of short stories many deal with themes common to Victorian fiction: love, marriage, money, domestic crises, and problems of society. Collins's interest in crime and a natural bent toward the unraveling of a mystery led him almost inadvertently toward the formula that culminated in the spectacular success of *The Woman in White* (1860) and *The Moonstone* (1868). Many of his lesser-known works before 1860 show signs of his developing talents for suspense and detection. After 1870 Collins regrettably turned away from the mystery formula and devoted himself for the most part to novels of social protest, in which the quality of his fiction sharply declined. Although his reputation rests chiefly upon *The Woman in White*, *The Moonstone*, and two other novels of the 1860s, *No Name* (1862) and *Armadale* (1866), many of Collins's other novels and stories also provide stimulating reading for today's mystery fans and at the same time give readers his own unique view of Victorian manners and morals.

THE LIFE

Wilkie Collins was a man of great personal charm, adored by his friends' children, a genial host and bon vivant, a lover of French wines and cuisine, an ardent theatergoer, and a man of generally unorthodox views. He was impatient of middle-class respectability, despised religious cant, and felt special compassion for fallen women. His sympathetic portraits of these "fallen leaves," as he titled one of his late novels, brought down upon him the wrath of the Mrs. Grundyites, whom he regarded with derision.

Nothing in Collins's upbringing would have forecast his adult character as a sophisticated man of the world. He was born in London on January 8, 1824, the son of William Collins, R.A., the distinguished landscape painter. Christened William Wilkie Collins, he later dropped the "William" in favor of the middle name given him after his godfather, the painter Sir David Wilkie. Far from growing up in a bohemian artist's household, as one might expect, Wilkie spent his childhood in an atmosphere of unimpeachable respectability. His father was a man of deeply felt religious faith, prudent in money matters, orderly in his habits, and somewhat prone to giving moral lectures to Wilkie and his younger brother Charles. That Wilkie ultimately rejected most of his father's principles testifies to his dislike of their austerity but does not necessarily indicate real animosity toward his father. Wilkie's *Memoirs* of his father gives glimpses of domestic felicity, of family expeditions, and of the young Wilkie delighting in walks with his father in which the painter's eye illuminated the surrounding objects of nature.[2]

When Wilkie was twelve, the family set off for a stay of two years in Italy, much to the delight of the imaginative boy, who adored all things Italian and especially enjoyed two years' remission from school. The private schools in London that he attended before and after the visit to Italy brought him no fond recollections. In later years, he always spoke deprecatingly of English education, insisting that he was bored at school and was often punished for bad behavior.[3] At seventeen, having apparently declined going to a university, Wilkie was placed in the office of a London tea broker, where he was equally restless and inattentive. After five years Wilkie was released from the tea trade and was entered by his father at Lincoln's Inn to study law. At that time young gentlemen might pay their fees, eat a few ritual dinners, and be called to the bar with very little actual knowledge of the law. Such was the case with Wilkie, who admired the profession but never practiced it. He introduced into his novels a long series of kindly family solicitors, but when he used legal problems in his plots he consulted experts, as he assures his readers in various prefaces.

Wilkie's real interest in these formative years was in his efforts at writing. He had a few short pieces accepted in magazines and was engaged upon a novel set in ancient Rome, after the fashion of Bulwer Lytton's *Last Days of Pompeii*, when his father died in 1847. Mr. Collins, having acquired over the years many wealthy and titled patrons, left his wife and sons with a comfortable income. Thus Wilkie was able to pursue a career in writing without financial worry. He set aside his novel to produce his *Memoirs* of his father, published in 1848 and well received by the critics. The Roman novel *Antonina* came out in 1850 to remarkably good reviews considering that its high-flown sentiment and verbosity make it almost unreadable today.

In the following year Collins was introduced to Charles Dickens and thus began the most important friendship of his life. The painter Augustus Egg recommended Wilkie for a part in the amateur production of Bulwer Lytton's *Not So Bad As We Seem* which Dickens was getting up to raise money for the actors' fund. Collins at once found himself in distinguished company, for the first performance took place at Devonshire House on May 16, 1851, in the presence of Queen Victoria and Prince Albert.[4] Dickens praised Collins's performance and took him along when the troupe toured the provinces. In 1853 Collins and Augustus Egg accompanied Dickens on a trip through

Switzerland and Italy, hilariously described in Dickens's letters to his family. Collins often joined the Dickens family on holidays at Boulogne, Paris, and elsewhere and was a frequent guest in their home.

Meanwhile Collins was contributing regularly to Dickens's weekly *Household Words* and later joined the editorial staff. The two writers often collaborated on Christmas stories and other pieces for *Household Words*, including a light-hearted account of their wanderings through Cumberland in search of story material, entitled *The Lazy Tour of Two Idle Apprentices*. Each influenced the other in certain respects. Collins's early fiction contains a number of Dickensian eccentrics and occasional passages of Dickensian rhetoric but these gradually disappeared as Collins's own voice matured. On the other hand, Dickens sometimes picked up from Collins ideas for plots or themes. A case in point is the play *The Frozen Deep*, which Collins wrote for Dickens's amateur players. In his preface to *A Tale of Two Cities* Dickens writes that it was when he was acting in this play with his children and friends that he "first conceived the main idea of this story." In the play two men on an Arctic expedition are in love with the same woman. Dickens, playing the role which was to become Sydney Carton, moved his audiences to tears with his intense portrayal of the man who sacrifices himself to save the life of his preferred rival. The background of the French Revolution may also have been suggested to Dickens by "Sister Rose," a Collins story that appeared in *Household Words* at the time Dickens was formulating ideas for his *Tale*. Apart from such specific instances, it seems likely that, as Collins's biographer Kenneth Robinson suggests, Collins's influence can be seen "in the increasing attention that Dickens pays to the plot in his last four or five novels, which display a tautness of construction not to be found in the earlier books."[5] Certainly by the time Dickens wrote *Edwin Drood* he was responding to the extraordinary success of Collins's *The Moonstone* in attempting a full-fledged mystery novel of his own.

In the course of time, Collins became Dickens's most intimate friend as well as a relation by marriage when his brother Charles married Dickens's daughter Kate. Dickens seemed to find in Wilkie Collins just that fun-loving spirit his restless and energetic nature craved, a companion always ready for an evening of theater, a lively dinner, or an excursion to anywhere the fancy dictated. In a characteristic letter to Collins in May 1857 Dickens wrote: "On Wednesday, sir—on Wednesday—if the mind can devise anything sufficiently in the style of sybarite Rome in the days of its culminating voluptuousness, I am your man."[6]

Their actual behavior may have been less licentious than it appears, but even allowing for Dickensian hyperbole it is clear that, when in the company of the broadminded and unconventional Collins, Dickens felt himself to be a free spirit. His passion for the actress Ellen Ternan began about this time, erupting into scandal when he published statements about his separation from his wife. Victorian society was accustomed to rumors of infidelities; gentlemen might have their mistresses so long as they were discreet. What could not be overlooked was public acknowledgment of domestic strife. In this crisis, Collins seems to have given his friend the kind of support he craved, while others who remonstrated with Dickens were never forgiven.

Collins was no doubt all the more tolerant of others because of his own irregular relationships with women. While remaining technically a bachelor all of his life, he lived with one woman for twenty-five years or more and had three children by another, referring to them as his "morganatic family." During his lifetime he maintained such official discretion that little was known about these relationships, except among his close friends, until well into the twentieth century. How all of this came about forms a mystery as intriguing as any of those in Collins's fiction, but one to which no omniscient detective can give us the solution in a closing chapter. Mystery fans may make their own guesses from the evidence available. Here are the facts as they came to be known.

In 1899, ten years after Collins's death, a biography of the painter John Everett Millais was published by Millais's son, in which Millais recalls a summer evening in the 1850s when he walked with Wilkie Collins and his brother Charley through the dimly lit streets of north London toward Millais's home in Gower Street. The young men had spent a pleasant evening at the Collins home near Regent's Park, where Mrs. Collins hospitably received her sons' friends. As they walked along in the moonlight,

> they were suddenly arrested by a piercing scream coming from the garden of a villa close at hand. It was evidently the cry of a woman in distress; and while pausing to con-

sider what they should do, the iron gate leading to the garden was dashed open, and from it came the figure of a young and very beautiful woman dressed in flowing white robes that shone in the moonlight. She seemed to float rather than run in their direction, and, on coming up to the three young men, she paused for a moment in an attitude of supplication and terror. Then, suddenly seeming to recollect herself, she suddenly moved on and vanished in the shadows cast upon the road.

"What a lovely woman!" was all Millais could say. "I must see who she is, and what is the matter," said Wilkie Collins, as, without a word he dashed off after her.[7]

The two friends waited in vain for Wilkie to return, and when they met the next day Wilkie seemed reluctant to talk of the incident. They did gather, however, that she "was a young lady of good birth and position, who had accidentally fallen into the hands of a man living in a villa in Regent's Park. There for many months he kept her prisoner under threats and mesmeric influence of so alarming a character that she dared not attempt to escape, until, in sheer desperation, she fled from the brute, who, with a poker in his hand, threatened to dash her brains out." Millais's account ends with the cryptic statement that "the woman's subsequent history, interesting as it is, is not for these pages." Who was this mysterious "woman in white" who appeared to Wilkie in the moonlight and whose story cannot be told?

A clue appeared in 1939, when Professor Clyde K. Hyder revealed that Wilkie Collins's will divided his estate between two women and their children. One of these was

Caroline Elizabeth Graves, whose death certificate describes her as the widow of George Robert Graves, and who is buried in Kensal Green Cemetery in London in the same grave with Wilkie Collins, although only his name is marked on the stone. That she is the same Caroline who lived with Collins is evidenced by her name appearing over a period of years in the Post Office Directory as occupying houses in which Collins is known to have lived.[8]

Another piece of evidence, also in 1939, appeared in the memoirs of Dickens's daughter Kate published by her friend Gladys Storey. Kate Perugini—she had remarried after the death of Charles Collins—repeated Millais's story of the meeting in the moonlight, stating that the original "woman in white" was named Caroline, a young woman of gentle birth who lived with Collins for many years. She then added that Caroline later married another man and that Collins attended the wedding, coming to visit Kate afterward to tell her all about it. Since she was Wilkie's sister-in-law at the time, she was in his confidence but unfortunately for future biographers she told no more.[9]

Since the records produced by Hyder showed Caroline living with Wilkie Collins at the time of his death, the story of the marriage was all the more puzzling. In 1951 Kenneth Robinson, in his excellent *Wilkie Collins: A Biography*, adds another piece of evidence, confirming Kate's story of the marriage. He cites records at St. Marylebone Parish Church of the marriage on October 4, 1868, between Caroline Elizabeth Graves, widow, and Joseph Charles Clow, son of a distiller, the witnesses being Collins's friend, Francis Carr Beard, and Caroline's daughter Harriette.[10] Yet within two years Caroline had returned to Collins. As Robinson states:

> Mystery surrounds Caroline's second marriage; from the moment that Joseph Clow signed the register as her husband, his name vanishes from our sight. Less than two years later, Wilkie inscribed a presentation copy of his new novel to "Mrs. George Graves," and though there is no record of a divorce it was as "widow of G. R. Graves," and not as the wife or widow of Joseph Clow, that Caroline was described at the time of her death. She returned to live with Wilkie early in the 70's and remained with him, as Mrs. Graves, until his death nearly 20 years later.[11]

Why did Caroline leave Collins to marry another man? We do not know. What we do know is that the other woman to whom Collins left half of his estate was Martha Rudd "Dawson," the mother of three children whom Collins names in his will as his own, and for whom he invented the name Dawson. The first child was born on July 14, 1869, exactly nine months after Caroline's marriage to Clow. It is easy enough to conjecture that Collins had formed a liaison with Martha that caused Caroline to leave him, but it may equally have happened that Collins sought Martha as consolation when Caroline planned to marry. His attendance at her wedding suggests compliance, but other evidence indicates that he was deeply distressed.

During the period after Caroline's marriage Collins did not take up residence with Martha, although she was already pregnant with his child, but lived instead for long periods with his friends the Lehmanns near Highgate, while working on his novel *Man and Wife*.[12] In a letter to Frederick Lehmann he mentions refusing invitations and keeping himself quiet "after this disaster," which may or may not refer to his domestic crisis.[13] A final puzzling feature of Collins's dual families is that Martha Rudd and her children lived at various residences in the neighborhood of Regent's Park within walking distance of Wilkie and Caroline's home.

We know very little about either Caroline or Martha, except for a few veiled references in letters. In 1860 Dickens wrote to a friend: "Wilkie has finished his White Woman (if he had done with his flesh-colored one, I should mention that too).[14] In letters to Collins, Dickens occasionally referred to Caroline's small daughter by a pet name: "Love to the Butler from her ancient partner in the card Trade. And kind regards to the Butler's mama."[15] Collins's letters to close friends sometimes mention Caroline and even more rarely his "morganatic family," but officially all was silence. Like George Eliot in a similar situation, Caroline could not be "received" in society; writers and artists visited freely but their wives could not call.

To summarize, the evidence seems to indicate that Caroline Graves was a "lady" who was not living with her husband—was he the man with the poker?—but who would under other circumstances have been socially suitable for marriage to Wilkie Collins. Except for the interval of her marriage to the elusive Joseph Clow, Caroline and Collins appear to have lived together very much as man and wife from some time in the 1850s until his death, regarding her daughter as their own child. They traveled together both at home and abroad, and Caroline was accepted by his intimate friends as his permanent companion.

The affair with Martha Rudd, whatever its inception, has the appearance of a more commonplace liaison. She continued to live "under his protection," in the Victorian phrase, and to give birth to his children even after she must have known of Caroline's return to his household. The conclusion is unavoidable that she accepted Caroline as his wife and herself as his mistress, regardless of the legalities of their position.

Thus some tantalizing questions are left unanswered: Was Martha the cause or the result of Caroline's marriage? What became of Joseph Clow? Under what circumstances did the two families coexist, living only a few streets apart? A biography of Collins by Nuel Pharr Davis which appeared in 1956 attempts to give some answers to these and other questions but proves to be unreliable. Davis fails to separate conjecture from truth, often quoting selected passages from the novels as if they were biographical fact.[16] Mystery fans, adhering to the detective code of fair play, may theorize freely, but until more evidence is uncovered the final answers remain elusive. Whatever the facts, Collins's bohemian view of life and his extraordinary flouting of Victorian standards of propriety lend a flavor of sophistication to his fiction which often shocked his more prudish critics but which makes his work appealing to today's readers.

Meanwhile, the decade of the 1860s saw Collins at the

peak of his literary powers. The popularity of *The Woman in White* and *The Moonstone* secured his position as one of the most acclaimed writers of his day. He was a member of the Athenaeum and other clubs and had a wide circle of friends, both literary and artisitc. Through his brother, the painter Charles Allston Collins, he knew the members of the Pre-Raphaelite group, including Millais, Holman Hunt, the Rossetti family, and others.

Collins was plagued throughout his adult life with recurring bouts of illness. As early as the 1850s he suffered from what his doctors called "rheumatic gout," which not only caused pain in the legs and feet but also attacked his eyes, causing severe inflammation. He began taking laudanum, a form of opium, to relieve the pain and eventually became addicted to the drug, although he seems never to have reached the depths of degradation suffered by DeQuincey or Coleridge. In intervals of good health, he maintained a vigorous literary and social life, traveled, coped with two mistresses—as we have seen—and even made a reading tour to America in 1873–74. While not as dramatic a performer as Dickens, whose renowned readings caused women to faint and strong men to weep, Collins's own quiet reading was much admired, and for his part, he was charmed by American friendliness and hospitality.

While Collins's final years were marred by ill health and declining powers, his novels continued to sell, although never at the level reached in the 1860s, and at his death in 1889 he was one of the most successful and beloved writers of his era.

EARLY WORKS

Nothing in Wilkie Collins's first published novel, the historical *Antonina*, gave promise of his future as a writer of mysteries, but among the ensuing works of the 1850s there are clear signs of his growing interest in crime and suspense. After keeping the pot boiling with a lighthearted travelogue, *Rambles Beyond Railways: or Notes in Cornwall taken Afoot* (1851), Collins tried his hand at a "Christmas Number" after the fashion of Dickens. *Mr. Wray's Cash-Box, or The Mask and the Mystery* (1852) is a trivially sentimental tale of Reuben Wray, an old actor whose passion for Shakespeare leads him to secretly take a cast from the poet's bust in the church in Stratford-upon-Avon. He keeps his relic hidden in a cashbox, believing that he has committed a crime for which he could be prosecuted. When thieves break in, tempted by the supposed cash in the box, the story of the cast is revealed and the local lawyer assures Reuben that taking the mask was not illegal. The chief interest for today's readers is that Collins gives away the plot in his introduction to the story. Throughout his writing career Collins had an unhappy compulsion to preface his works with explanatory remarks, often attesting to their authenticity, and later indulging in challenges or replies to critics. Here, his introduction tells the reader that a stonemason did in fact take a mask from Shakespeare's bust and later learned that his act was not criminal, as he had feared. Since this anecdote destroys any "mystery" in the story, it is clear that Collins's interest in verisimilitude in this early work outweighed his concern for the mystery element. He was still a long way from the beautifully crafted suspense of his major fiction.

In 1852 Collins was at work on *Basil*, his first serious novel in a contemporary setting, using the classic Victorian theme of marriage between persons of different social classes. Basil, the second son of "one of the most ancient families in England," sees a beautiful girl on an omnibus and falls in love with her at first sight, a favorite motif throughout Collins's fiction. When Basil learns that Margaret Sherwin's father is a dry-goods merchant, his reason tells him at once that his father, who prizes the family tradition as a sacred trust, could never accept his son's marriage with the daughter of a shopkeeper, but Basil is stricken with the passion of first love. He does not see Margaret's obvious superficiality, nor is he warned off by Mr. Sherwin's mean and grasping nature and his new-rich pretensions to gentility. The naive Basil enters into a secret marriage with Margaret, promising her father to wait a year before they live together as man and wife. Basil visits Margaret daily, enchanted by her beauty, and relying on the apparent friendship of Mr. Sherwin's clerk, Robert Mannion, to aid him in his visits.

Collins shows a budding talent for planting clues by giving a series of apparently trivial incidents that lead to the revelation of Margaret's duplicity and Mannion's villainy. The scene of betrayal is excellently done but shocked the prudish by its explicit account of the adulterous tryst. Had Margaret been an admirable girl, Collins would no doubt have attacked society's strictures against "marrying out of one's class," but in *Basil* his theme is more moral than social—the father and daughter are condemned not because of their social status but because they are morally depraved.

In his preface to *Basil* Collins sets forth some principles for the writing of fiction. He aims to use "the Actual" and to shed "the light of Reality" wherever possible by using commonplace settings such as the lovers' meeting on an omnibus, "the very last place . . . which the artifices of sentimental writing would sanction." At the same time, the preface adds that everyday realities alone are not enough, that "the Novel and the Play are twin-sisters in the family of Fiction", in short, that dramatic incidents beyond the reader's own experience may also be defended in order to "fix his interest and excite his suspense." The second half of *Basil* does indeed become more melodramatic, beginning with the disfigurement of Mannion and following to its ultimate conclusion his implacable desire for revenge against Basil.

To the reader, the first part of the novel with its realistic incidents is more effectively suspenseful and certainly more appealing than the closing scenes of horror. The treatment of Basil's first love and its anguish has the ring of personal experience, although no evidence exists to supply the particulars. In his best work, Collins was to adhere for the most part to his principle of realism, while his weakest fiction often proved to be that in which excessively melodramatic elements flourished.

In his third novel, *Hide and Seek* (1854), Collins for the first time developed what was intended to be a mystery plot. While the novel is in other respects entertaining, as a mystery its devices are so transparent that it is of interest chiefly as an experiment in the form. Subtitled *The Mystery of Mary Grice*, the story recounts the death of the unwed mother of the title, whose infant daughter is adopted by a kindly couple connected with a circus.[17] The child becomes a deaf mute through an accident, is mistreated by the circus owner, and is adopted by Valentine Blyth, a London artist of no talent but of limitless virtue. Some twenty years later, Mary's vagabond brother, Matthew Grice, returns from his wanderings to seek revenge upon his sister's seducer. Coincidences abound: Matthew meets young Zachary Thorpe, who takes him to the Blyth home where he instantly recognizes the adopted daughter as Mary's child; he sees a hair bracelet there that matches the description of one belonging to his sister; and the final identification of the seducer strains credulity beyond the average reader's tolerance. Since most of the elements of the mystery are apparent long before they are revealed in the novel, it is clear that in *Hide and Seek* Collins was making a trial run through a fictional form still a long way from maturity.

Despite its weaknesses in suspense, *Hide and Seek* offers some indication of Collins's development as a writer. Mary Grice is the first of Collins's sympathetic portraits of the fallen woman, and in her aunt Joanna Grice we see the first of the religious hypocrites whom Collins bitterly condemns. The influence of Dickens is strong in this early novel. Mat the frontiersman, while outwardly a Natty Bumpo, is a Dickensian eccentric in habits and speech;

Valentine Blyth shares the cherubic benevolence of Mr. Brownlow, who came to the rescue of Oliver Twist; even the deaf mute takes her place with Dickens's large cast of characters with physical handicaps; and Mr. Tatt, the greedy lawyer, no doubt reflects Dickens's scorn for a profession that Collins later presents in a most favorable light.

Occasionally Collins lapses into rhapsodic prose from the very school of sentimental fiction he deplored in his Preface to *Basil*, as in this passage apostrophizing the fates on little Mary's deafness:

> Ah, woful [sic] sight! so lovely, yet so piteous to look on! Shall she never hear kindly human voices, the song of birds, the pleasant murmur of the trees again? . . . Oh! Angel of Judgment! hast thou snatched her hearing and her speech from this little child, to abandon her in helpless affliction to such profanation as she now undergoes? Oh, Spirit of mercy! how long thy white-winged feet have tarried on their way to this innocent sufferer. . . . (Chapter 3)

and so on for a lengthy paragraph. Happily, such rhetoric almost never occurs in Collins's subsequent fiction. Dickens, with his compensating genius, may be forgiven such passages, but Collins's strength lies in his straightforward and unaffected prose, as in the following passage describing the funeral of Joanna Grice, whose narrow principles had caused her niece's death:

> When Mary Grice died, a fugitive and an outcast, the clown's wife and the Irish girl who rode in the circus wept

for her, stranger though she was, as they followed her coffin to the poor-corner of the churchyard. When Joanna Grice died in the place of her birth, among the townspeople with whom her whole existence had been passed, every eye was tearless that looked on her funeral procession; the two strangers who made part of it gossiped pleasantly as they rode after the hearse about the news of the morning; and the sole surviving member of her family, whom chance had brought to her door on her burial-day, stood aloof from the hired mourners and moved not a step to follow her to the grave. (Chapter 13)

Both the note of cynicism in the hired mourners and the balanced rhetoric without a trace of sentimental flourish are characteristic of the direction in which Collins's style developed as his artistry matured.

In the 1850s Collins regularly wrote short stories and other pieces for periodicals, mostly for Dickens's *Household Words*. In 1856 he published a collection of six of these stories entitled *After Dark*, loosely connected by a frame narrative about a young artist who works desperately to support his wife and two small children. Although his own father ultimately became a distinguished and financially successful painter, Collins recalled his early struggles and stated in his preface that it was his object to "ask some sympathy for the joys and sorrows of a poor traveling portrait-painter."

The stories in *After Dark* contain a number of features pointing to Collins's development as a mystery writer. "A Terribly Strange Bed," a story which has frequently been included in anthologies, recounts the adventure of a young Englishman who wins a large amount of money at a seedy gambling house in Paris and is then drugged and put to bed in an upstairs chamber of the establishment, where he locks himself in. He awakens in the night to find the top of the fourposter descending silently upon him and avoids suffocation in the nick of time. The story is done very much in the manner of Edgar Allan Poe's horror tales, dwelling upon the young man's extreme terror.

While there is no mystery in the plot itself, the story gives an interesting glimpse of the efficiency and enthusiasm of the French police, who functioned in the manner prescribed by Vidocq and his successors at the Surêté. When the young man in the story escapes through the window and rushes to the nearest prefecture, the local officer and his men set off with him to the gaming house, where they take up floor boards, reveal the mechanism of the murderous bed, and arrest the inmates of the house, conducting the whole episode with the gusto of men who enjoy their work and go about it with skill.

The title of the second story in the collection, "A Stolen Letter," sounds like another Poe imitation, but except for the title the story bears little resemblance to "The Purloined Letter." Unlike Poe's story of political intrigue in the French court and the detecting powers of the brilliant Auguste Dupin, Collins's story is a lighthearted and charming little tale set in rural England and having as its detective a brash but kindly young lawyer, Mr. Boxsious. He retrieves an incriminating letter for his client with the aid of young Tom, his fourteen-year-old office boy, whose cleverness in tailing the suspect while innocently eating pastries or loitering about unseen makes him a prototype for one of Sherlock Holmes's Baker Street Irregulars. The letter is not found, like Poe's, in an open and obvious place but has been hidden away and is found through a rather primitive little code. Only in the end does Collins borrow a device from Poe as Boxsious leaves a flippant message in the place from which the missing letter was retrieved.

The story "The Yellow Mask" again shows Collins trading in Poe's territory but in this case without the American writer's admirable economy. Set in Pisa, the story recounts at great length the love of a young nobleman for a simple girl of the people, the machinations of a priest bent upon restoring the nobleman's family wealth to the church, and the attempted revenge of an evil woman who feels herself scorned. Unfortunately the characters are stereotyped and their motives unconvincing. The final scene, a masked ball suggestive of Poe's "Masque of the Red Death" without the plague, is intended to convey horror as the woman wearing the yellow mask tears it off and reveals the face beneath, but the effect is only partially successful.

Two stories in *After Dark* are set in the period of the French Revolution and suggest that Collins was experimenting with historical fiction in the vein of Sir Walter Scott. "Gabriel's Marriage" is a grim little story of an intended crime in a family of peasants in Brittany and of the priest who risks his life to hold services during the time when religion was outlawed. A more important novella-length story, "Sister Rose," set during the Reign of Terror, gives a haunting picture of a brother who devotes his life to his sister, trying to protect her during the period of her disastrous marriage to a man who becomes a tool of the revolutionary regime. The influence on Dickens's *A Tale of Two Cities* can be seen in the lists of those condemned to the guillotine, the incidents within the prison concerning those awaiting execution, and the dramatic rescue of the brother and sister, as well as in the theme of regeneration through self-sacrifice which had so impressed Dickens in *The Frozen Deep*.[18] Just as historical fiction was a departure for Dickens from his usual mode, so Collins was more at home using contemporary settings and seldom returned to history in his subsequent fiction.

The only story in *After Dark* not previously published, "The Lady of Glenwith Grange," is perhaps the most artistically successful of the group. The character of Ida Welwyn is nicely developed through the eyes of the narrator, a gentleman neighbor who admires her over a period of years but cannot press his suit because she has devoted her life to rearing the infant sister left in her charge by her dying mother. A genuine mystery of identity develops in this story and Collins's handling of the suspense is decidedly superior to his technique in *Hide and Seek*. There is no attempt at Dickensian joviality; the tone is somber and the relationships are treated with delicacy reminiscent of the more effective portions of *Basil*.

If a writer's progress sometimes moves in a spiral pattern rather than a constantly ascending line, then Collins's next novel, *The Dead Secret* (1857) represents a low point preceding the spectacular accomplishment of *The Woman in White*. The actual substance of the plot of *The Dead Secret* would comprise a good short story, so that Collins seems to have fallen victim here to the publishing tradition of his day which required a novel to fill two or three fat volumes for the benefit of the circulating libraries. Today's wafer-thin mystery novels would not have prospered in such a market, except as periodical items, for which the pay was less than for the book. Since Collins was at all times a conscientious craftsman, it is unlikely that he was intentionally padding, but today's reader is likely to feel that the material is unduly stretched. Nevertheless, the novel has redeeming features—a lively and charming heroine in Rosamund Treverton and some fine use of setting in remote Cornwall, as it then was.

As another trial run for Collins's developing interest in mystery fiction, *The Dead Secret* must have been a valuable object lesson. He was attempting, as he did in *Hide and Seek*, to sustain a "secret" throughout the length of the novel and was even less successful here than before. Contemporary reviewers noted this at once, complaining that "*The Dead Secret* is no secret to a numerous class of readers" and that "the secret is plainly discernible in the very opening of the book."[19] Nevertheless he was praised for his ingenuity and "his keen, spirited writing."[20] The critics' assessment of his failure in sustaining suspense must have goaded Collins into rethinking his technique, for it is as a master of suspense that he emerges in his fiction of the 1860s.

In 1859 Collins published another collection of short stories all of which had appeared in periodicals in the preceding four years. The title of the collection, *The Queen of*

Hearts, derives from the frame story of three elderly retired brothers—a clergyman, a doctor, and a lawyer—
who must entertain a young lady for six weeks and who
devise a sort of *Arabian Nights* series of evening stories to
keep her entertained. This contrivance is saved from mediocrity by Collins's deft portrait of the charming and
spirited Jessie Yelverton, fondly dubbed "The Queen of
Hearts," and her disarming affection for her three ancient
admirers. Jessie and her predecessor Rosamund in *The
Dead Secret* are two early examples of the attractive young
women who later become a hallmark of Collins's fiction.
Dickens, for all his genius, was never able to create a
"good" girl who had much spirit; the Rose Maylies and
Agnes Wickfields, the little Doras and Dorrits, are pleasant but a trifle insipid, whereas Collins's heroines are often bold, strong-willed, and independent.

A case in point is the young country girl in "The Siege of
the Black Cottage," the first story in the collection. Left
alone overnight in a lonely cottage on the moor, she feels
secure until a pair of miscreants attack the cottage, knowing that a large sum of money is hidden there. Bessie cou-
rageously defies them and eventually makes her escape
with the money in her bosom and her beloved cat in her
apron.

The stories in *The Queen of Hearts* generally show growth
in Collins's artistic powers. Some, like "The Family Secret," "Fauntleroy," and "The Parson's Scruple," are slight
but entertaining, and the latter story is interesting as the
first example of Collins's attack upon English and Scottish
divorce law. Others are essentially horror stories. In this

group "The Dream Woman" uses the device of a terrifying dream which later comes true. Isaac, a rural laborer, sees in a dream a woman raising a knife to stab him as he lies in bed. He reports this to his mother, who writes down his description of the woman: "Light gray eyes . . . with a droop in the left eyelid; flaxen hair, with a gold-yellow streak in it; white arms, with a down upon them, little lady's hand, with a reddish look about the finger nails; clasp-knife with a buckhorn handle." Years later the bachelor Isaac meets and marries the dream woman, against his mother's warnings, and of course lives to regret it. He escapes death but is forever haunted by the dream. Such a story naturally invites Freudian criticism. The interpretation offered by N. P. Davis, equating the protective mother with Collins's own mother Harriet and the baleful dream wife with Caroline Graves[21] seems totally unsupported by the evidence of Collins's life. It is more likely that in the dream motif Collins was using a popular device for titillating his readers' fondness for the eerie and one that he uses a number of times in his fiction, most notably in his novel *Armadale*.

In two other horror stories in *The Queen of Hearts* Collins shows his talent for hair-raising episodes. The young hero of "The Dead Hand" finds himself sharing a room at an inn with a "dead" man whose hand moves. In "Mad Monkton" Collins departs from "the Actual" and writes a genuine ghost story in which the ghost is not explained away. There is some detection in the story as well, but horror predominates in scenes like that in which a decomposing body is described in grisly detail. Collins later on ventured again into the realm of the ghost story in a novella entitled *The Haunted Hotel* (1878), but for the most part he worked in a realistic mode.

Putting aside ghosts and the ghoulish, the remaining three stories in *The Queen of Hearts* show Collins emerging as a full-fledged writer of detective fiction. All three stories point significantly to his growing interest in methods of detecting a crime and to his increasing skill in keeping the reader in suspense. In the first of these, "Anne Rodway," Anne's diary records the death of her friend Mary, Anne's suspicion that Mary was murdered, and her pursuit of a series of clues that lead to the arrest of the guilty man. Accordingly, Anne has been appropriately dubbed the first lady detective by some historians of detective fiction.[22] In addition to its mystery formula, the story has social significance through its exposure of the plight of young seamstresses like Anne and Mary living in appalling poverty in a London slum. In a letter to Collins in 1856 Dickens expressed his admiration for the story: "I cannot tell you what a high opinion I have of 'Anne Rodway' . . . . Apart from the genuine force and beauty of the little narrative, and the admirable personation of the girl's identity and point of view, it is done with an amount of honest pains and devotion to the work which few men have better reason to appreciate than I."[23] Collins shared with Dickens a deep concern for the condition of London's poor, and Mary's accidental death at the hands of a drunken ruffian comments movingly upon society's apparent indifference to such tragedies.

In the 1850s Collins shared Dickens's admiration for the London Detective Police, and in "The Biter Bit," another detective story in *The Queen of Hearts*, Collins pays that group a pleasant compliment. Told through a series of letters, the story concerns a robbery case a chief inspector of the detective department has assigned to a new man on the force, a conceited lawyer's clerk who believes that he can dazzle the stodgy professionals and solve the case with ease. The story demonstrates the problem of all police departments from that day to this of securing qualified people at relatively low pay. In the frame story that introduces "The Biter Bit" the narrator comments on the efforts of the new department to increase its members by recruiting from among the lawyers' clerks, many of whom served as private investigators on behalf of clients. The speaker, a lawyer himself

> felt certain that the really experienced clerks intrusted with conducting investigations and hunting up lost evidence, were too well paid and too independently situated in their various offices to care about entering the ranks of the Detective Police, and submitting themselves to the rigid discipline of Scotland Yard, and I ventured to predict that the inferior clerks only, whose discretion was not to be trusted, would prove to be the men who volunteered for detective employment.

One of these "inferior clerks" was demonstrated in the character of Matthew Sharpin in "The Biter Bit." In this clever and amusing story, Sharpin's letters to the chief inspector report his "progress" on the case, recounting his absurd following up of false clues and arriving at mistaken solutions. Given Sharpin's confused account as their source, the chief inspector and his sergeant demonstrate the efficiency of true professionals by laying hands on the real culprit without further ado. The story implies that bumblers like Sharpin are promptly weeded out of the system, and that despite their modest pay, the detective officers must meet the high standards of Scotland yard.

The final story in *The Queen of Hearts,* the excellent novella entitled "A Plot in Private Life," is the most fully developed detective story yet to come from Collins's pen. The story contains a remarkable number of features that have become common to twentieth-century mystery fiction, including a disappearing husband, a bloodstained nightgown but no body, the arrest of two suspects who are proved innocent, and an incomparable detective in the lawyer's clerk, Mr. Dark, whose jaunty self-confidence never flags. The portrait of Dark owes a good deal to Dickens's Inspector Bucket in *Bleak House* (1852), with his brisk manner and his capacity for eliciting information from the unwary. Having given us an example of an "inferior clerk" as detective in "The Biter Bit," Collins now reveals his opposite number, one of the "really experienced clerks." Mr. Dark is first described by the young manservant William, who narrates the story:

> I had expected, from his master's description, to see a serious, sedate man, rather sly in his looks, and rather reserved in his manner. To my amazement, this practiced hand at delicate investigations was a brisk, plump, jolly little man, with a comfortable double chin, a pair of bright

black eyes, and a big bottle-nose of the true groggy red color. He wore a suit of black, and a limp, dingy white cravat; took snuff perpetually out of a very large box; walked with his hands crossed behind his back; and looked, upon the whole, much more like a parson of free-and-easy habits than a lawyer's clerk.

William, like an admiring Dr. Watson, is constantly astonished at Dark's ingenuity. He has never seen "the like of him for making intimate friends of total strangers at the shortest notice." Even in Scotland Dark elicits information from the cautious Scots, "twisting them round his finger as he pleased."

Having solved the first disappearance of the husband, Dark returns to London but tells William that the case is not over. When the husband disappears for the second time, and the innocent William and his mistress are accused of his murder, Collins sustains the reader's suspense by producing Mr. Dark with his crucial witness at the dramatic climax of the hearing before the justice. After the culprit is revealed and order is restored by the release of the innocents, Dark then engages in a lengthy flashback to William, recounting the steps by which he unraveled the mystery. Each clue is analyzed and explained to the admiring William in a finale that has since become a formula ending for the classic detective story.

THE WOMAN IN WHITE

The instantaneous popular success of *The Woman in White* made Collins a celebrity. As the weekly installments appeared in Dickens's new magazine *All the Year Round* from November 1859 to August 1860, people gathered around the doors of the office to get their copies hot off the press. No dinner party was complete without guesses about the next developments in the story. All sorts of products were labeled "Woman in White," from cloaks and bonnets to perfumes and toilet articles, while music publishers joined the parade with "Woman in White" waltzes and quadrilles.[24] The circulation of *All the Year Round*, which had done extremely well with Dickens's *A Tale of Two Cities*, soared to even higher figures during the run of *The Woman in White*. The story was equally popular in America, where it ran in *Harper's Magazine* during the same period. When it came out in book form, the sales were phenomenal on both sides of the Atlantic. Collins's contemporaries were entranced: Dickens praised its artistry, Thackeray sat up all night to finish it, Edward Fitzgerald named his boat the *Marian Halcombe*, Gladstone couldn't put it down, and Prince Albert adored it. The novel was later adapted for the stage, where it was a hit on both sides of the Atlantic.

The ingenuity of the plot alone would guarantee the popularity of *The Woman in White*. A young artist, Walter Hartright, meets a strange young woman named Anne Catherick, who speaks vaguely of the Fairlies of Limmeridge Hall in Cumberland at the very time that Walter is on his way there to take a post as drawing master. Soon after his arrival in Cumberland, Walter falls in love with his pupil, Laura Fairlie, only to learn that she has consented to honor her father's dying wish that she marry his friend Sir Percival Glyde. Her affectionate half sister, Marian Halcombe, realizes that Laura returns Walter's love and urges her to break off the engagement, but the pressures from her uncle and from Sir Percival himself are too strong for the fragile Laura, and the marriage takes place. By the terms of the marriage settlement, if Laura dies before her twenty-first birthday, the bulk of her enormous fortune goes to her husband, with a generous legacy to an aunt, the wife of an Italian named Count Fosco. After the honeymoon, Sir Percival and his bride return to England to live at Blackwater Park, his estate in Hampshire, accompanied by the Count and Countess Fosco. Marian Halcombe comes to make her home with her sister and is appalled at Sir Percival's contemptuous treatment of his wife. When Marian recovers from a severe illness and learns that Laura has been taken to London and reportedly died there, she suspects foul play and calls upon Walter Hartright to aid her in unmasking the culprits. In the unfolding of the mystery, Collins generates the kind of suspense which keeps his reader agog until the final chapter.

The central idea for *The Woman in White* came from a book which Collins picked up in Paris while strolling about with Dickens one day. Maurice Méjan's *Recueil des causes célèbres*, an extensive collection of French criminal cases, proved to be a rich source for Collins's plot material. In the case of the Marquise de Douhault, Méjan recounts that the lady's brother had seized her estates in 1787 and had then detained her in an asylum under an assumed name.[25] Although she escaped, she was never able to regain her legal rights. The account mentions that the Marquise was wearing a white dress both when she came to the asylum and when she left, a fact suggestive of Walter Hartright's memorable meeting with Anne Catherick on the night of her escape from the asylum in Hampstead:

> There, in the middle of the broad, bright high-road—
> there, as if it had that moment sprung out of the earth or
> dropped from the heaven—stood the figure of a solitary
> Woman, dressed from head to foot in white garments, her
> face bent in grave inquiry on mine, her hand pointing to
> the dark cloud over London, as I faced her.[26]

Thus there may have been a dual source for the title of Collins's novel—both the white dress of Madame de Douhault and the dramatic event in Collins's own life when Caroline Graves, clothed in white, fled from the villa in London and Collins came to her rescue.

The story of *The Woman in White* is told through a series of narrators, an ingenious innovation for controlling the information given to the reader. As Collins explains in the preamble to the novel, each narrator is permitted to report only the facts within his or her own experience, just as "the story of an offence [sic] against the laws is told in Court by more than one witness." The method contributes to the sense of authenticity through the testimony of the witnesses, at the same time helping to solve the perennial problem of the mystery writer in limiting the amount of information given to the reader.

Collins uses a number of devices in *The Woman in White* to sustain the reader's suspense. Sometimes he lays a trail of apparent answers, each of which proves to be more complex than it would initially appear to be. For example, Walter Hartright, in his role as amateur detective, learns that Sir Percival Glyde fears the exposure of a dread secret in his life. When Anne Catherick first expresses to Walter her hatred of Sir Percival and refers to her "misfortune," Walter (and the reader) guess that Sir Percival was Anne's seducer, but this too-easy solution to the secret is quickly rejected. To Walter's delicate question, Anne's response reflects the symbolic purity of her white garments: "She looked up at me," reports Walter, "with the artless bewilderment of a child. . . . No words that ever were spoken could have assured me, as her look and manner now assured me, that the motive which I had assigned . . . was plainly and distinctly the wrong one. That doubt, at any rate, was now set at rest; but the very removal of it opened a new prospect of uncertainty" (p. 88). Walter later uncovers facts that seem to point to Glyde as the seducer of Mrs. Catherick and hence the father of Anne, and again the reader feels that this is a simple—but disappointing—solution to Glyde's great secret. Walter promptly expresses the same thought: "Was this common, too common, story of a man's treachery and a woman's frailty the key to the secret which had been the life-long terror of Sir Percival Glyde?" (p. 432)

Walter's investigations then lead to a more complex solution which proves to be as wrong as the earlier guesses. Mrs. Catherick's terror at the mention of the church vestry suggests that she was Glyde's accomplice in a crime committed there. Walter's reflections are plausible but inaccurate: "What had been the nature of the crime? Surely there was a contemptible side to it, as well as a dangerous side, or Mrs. Catherick would not have repeated my own words, referring to Sir Percival's rank and power, with such marked disdain as she had certainly displayed" (p. 456). The real clue to the mystery lies in this very scorn of Glyde's "rank and power" but Collins has once more whisked his magician's kerchief over the scene before finally revealing the solution. This technique of artfully deceiving the reader into a series of naive suppositions has become a staple for Collins's successors in mystery fiction but few have surpassed this first master of the genre.

Another of Collins's devices in the novel might be called "deceptive foreshadowing." In the opening chapter, when Walter's volatile Italian friend Pesca declares that he now has the chance to repay Walter for having saved him from drowning, the repayment appears to be Pesca's obtaining for Walter the post of drawing master at Limmeridge. Yet in the end, when the reader has forgotten Pesca, his reappearance not only brilliantly completes a structural pattern but gives double meaning to the foreshadowed "repayment," for it is Pesca who exposes Fosco's betrayal of the blood brotherhood of the Italian terrorist group and thereby supplies Walter with the final piece of the puzzle.

The device of "deceptive misinformation," to invent another phrase, appears in the supposition that poor Anne Catherick knows Sir Percival's dread secret. In the novel it seems so unlikely that the icily controlled Mrs. Catherick would have told her daughter anything at all that it comes as a relief to the reader to learn that indeed she did not. Anne merely knew enough to suspect that there *was* a secret and for that alone Sir Percival had her put away. This device became a favorite with writers like Agatha Christie, whose characters sometimes "know something but don't know what they know," sounding like direct descendants of Anne Catherick.

Finally, the term "buried information," may be used to describe a device which has become standard in the classic detective story. A vital clue is "buried" in what appears to be the idle talk of a non-essential character. In *The Woman in White* Collins uses this expertly in the crucial scene in which the old parish clerk, while unlocking the church vestry and showing Walter the parish registery, chatters away about the former parish clerk, the solicitor who kept a copy of the register in his office lest the original be lost or destroyed:

> "He used to say . . . 'Why can't I make other people as careful as I am myself? Some of these days there will be an accident happen, and when the register's lost, then the parish will find out the value of my copy.' He used to take his pinch of snuff after that, and look about him as bold as a lord. Ah! the like of him for doing business isn't easy to find now. You may go to London and and not match him, even *there*. Which year did you say, sir? Eighteen hundred and what?"
>
> "Eighteen hundred and four," I replied, mentally resolving to give the old man no more opportunities of talking, until my examination of the register was over. (p. 462)

The reader regards this garrulous rustic as a bit of amusing local color, dismissing him as lightly as Walter does, until the existence of the copy proves to be the vital clue to the false entry in the church register.

No matter how ingeniously constructed a plot may be, however, the success of a story must rest upon its characters, as Collins himself notes in his preface to the 1861 edition of *The Woman in White:* "I have always held the old-fashioned opinion that the primary object of a work of fiction should be to tell a story; and I have never believed that the novelist who properly performed this first condition of his art, was in danger, on that account, of neglecting the delineation of character . . . for the only narrative which can lay a strong hold on the attention of readers is a narrative which interests them about men and women."

That Collins fulfilled the promise of his preface is amply demonstrated in the richness of the novel's characters. The incomparable Count Fosco is still perhaps the most brilliantly portrayed villain in mystery fiction. The otherwise clear-headed Marian initially falls under the spell of his charm, with sexual overtones that Collins could only hint at in those days of Victorian prudery. Marian's diary records that although Fosco is immensely fat and nearly sixty, he has attracted her against her will. "He has that quiet deference, that look of pleased, attentive interest in listening to a woman . . . which we can none of us resist," and his "unfathomable grey eyes" have a "cold, clear, beautiful, irresistible glitter in them which forces me to look at him, and yet causes me sensations, when I do look, which I would rather not feel" (p. 197). The Count is often so witty, cynical, and amusing that the reader, like Marian, is beguiled by him and must forcibly remember that this man who adores his little mice and talks so lovingly to his birds has indeed conceived and carried out the plan to incarcerate Laura in an asylum in order to get her money.

Marian Halcombe is a splendid character in her own right—intelligent, strong-willed, and resourceful. The roles of heroine and villain are doubled in the novel: Laura is the alter ego of Marian as Sir Percival is of Fosco. Marian's plain face and active nature are the obverse of Laura's beauty and passivity, and the two together uphold the principles of goodness and truth. Fosco and Sir Percival represent the corresponding forces of evil in their double roles, with Fosco's lethal geniality the counterpart of Sir Percival's vacillating surliness.

The minor characters are equally memorable. The countess rolls Fosco's cigarettes in slavish devotion; Mrs. Catherick waits each day for the clergyman's bow; and the hypochondriac Frederick Fairlie refuses to stir on behalf of anyone in the world but himself. It is worth noting that Fairlie's eccentricities are essential to the plot, for a healthy uncle with normal protective feelings would have rescued his niece and prevented the ensuing tragedy.

Certain features of *The Woman in White* suggest parallels in Robert Browning's great dramatic poem, *The Ring and the Book*, which appeared in 1869, a decade after Collins's novel. Both stories are based upon actual criminal cases from Continental sources. Like Collins's casual discovery of the Méjan casebook, Browning chanced upon the *Yellow Book* while strolling in Florence one day and found the dramatic account of the seventeeth-century trial of Count Guido for the murder of his wife Pompilia. The pregnant seventeen-year-old Pompilia had fled from her husband's cruelty with the aid of a young priest. Seeking revenge, Guido and his henchmen murdered Pompilia's stepparents and inflicted twenty-two stab wounds on the girl herself, but she survived long enough to identify her attackers. Guido based his defense on the accusation that Pompilia and the priest were lovers, but they were exonerated and Guido was convicted of the crime and executed after his appeal to the Pope was denied.

Like Collins, Browning used a series of narrators in *The Ring and the Book*, each speaker recounting in a dramatic monologue his or her version of the events of the murder story. The technique of using multiple narrators, each revealing his own idiosyncrasies in the course of giving testimony about a crime, may well have been suggested to Browning by Collins's innovative device in *The Woman in White*. A further similarity in the two works is the theme of the rescue of an innocent woman who has been victimized by an evil man. This was a theme dear to the heart of Browning, who in his own life had rescued Elizabeth Barrett from her repressive father, and equally so to Collins, who had rescued Caroline Graves from apparently imminent danger. Both Collins and Browning give an essentially romantic treatment to their crime stories, each condemning the loveless marriage contracted for gain, in which the woman is the innocent tool of forces outside her control.

In *The Woman in White* the theme of the innocent victim generates social as well as moral commentary. Collins often champions the cause of women in his fiction. While retaining many of the conventional attitudes of his day toward women as the weaker but nobler sex, he attacks the complacency of a society that affords women little legal protection. In *The Woman in White* he makes a strong case for granting married women control of their own money apart from the community property of the marriage. Laura is exploited largely because of the legal powers invested in Sir Percival as her husband. Anne Catherick, another victim of exploitation, illustrates the ease with which people could be shut away in asylums without official protection. While the conditions were at least humane in the private sanatorium where Anne (and later Laura) were placed, Collins returns to the theme in a later novel (*Jezebel's Daughter*, 1880) where he attacks the conditions in public asylums.

With *The Woman in White* Collins moved as a writer from apprentice to full-fledged artist. His early attempts at suspense in *Hide and Seek* and *The Dead Secret* matured as it were overnight into a flawlessly constructed novel in which nothing is extraneous and motivation grows out of character as well as circumstance. Symbol and setting are deftly handled. For example, when Marian Halcombe goes to Blackwater Park to await Laura's return from her wedding trip, she finds a little wounded spaniel in the old boathouse by the lake. The ominous setting of the fir plantation, the brackish and shrunken lake, and the decaying boathouse, all of which play a vital part in the events of the novel, are impressively done. Marian gathers up the little dog in her skirt, oblivious of bloodstains, and takes him back to the house, but despite her efforts she cannot save him. In an effective use of symbol the death of the spaniel forebodes the evil that is generated at Blackwater Park and Marian's failure to act as protector of Laura. But the little dog has more than mere symbolic significance: he is Mrs. Catherick's dog and thus plays his small part in the story just as every incident, no matter how trivial, contributes to the intricate structure of the novel.

Did Collins know that he was writing the first full-fledged mystery novel in English when he wrote *The Woman in White?* Probably not. But by writing a love story with a moral fable and adding layer upon layer of suspense, he created the happiest of combinations, a novel of first quality which was also a spectacular best-seller and which set a pattern for future generations of writers.

NO NAME AND *ARMADALE*

After the success of *The Woman in White* Collins did not immediately attempt to repeat the formula of that novel. In *No Name* (1862) he turned to a social theme—attacking the English law which barred illegitimate children from inheriting property—and to a different mode of suspense. Unlike *The Woman in White, No Name* does not depend upon the revelation of a series of secrets but derives its suspense instead from the heroine's pursuit of vengeance.

Although he never practiced law, Collins reveled in legal tangles in his fiction. Like the complexities of wills and marriage settlements in *The Woman in White*, the events in *No Name* arise from the fact that children who were born to a couple out of wedlock remained illegitimate under the law even though the parents subsequently married. Inheritance by such children must be secured through a will executed after the marriage has taken place. In the novel, the parents of Magdalen and Norah Vanstone had lived happily together for many years as man and wife, knowing that Mr. Vanstone's early and disastrous marriage was still valid. When news of the wife's death reached them, they promptly went off to London to be married. Unfortunately, the family lawyer, Mr. Pendril, was abroad at the time, and it was not until his return some months later that they learned the marriage invalidated Vanstone's earlier will. Vanstone sent for the lawyer to come at once to his country estate to draw up a new will, but before Mr. Pendril arrived, Vanstone was killed in a railway accident and Mrs. Vanstone died in childbirth, survived by an infant son who lived only a few hours. Vanstone's fortune of some eighty thousand pounds thus passed to the infant son (since the mother had died intestate) and thence to the next of kin, leaving the beloved daughters of the Vanstones penniless. (Had Mr. Pendril instructed Vanstone how to make a holographic will—one totally in his own handwriting—the situation would have been averted, but one can scarcely fault Mr. Pendril for not anticipating such a series of disasters.)

Collins's complaint, expressed by Mr. Pendril in the novel, is that the "more merciful and Christian law of other countries, which allows the marriage of the parents to make the children legitimate, has no mercy on *these* children." The law of England which denies them this right "in the names of morality and religion," has left these innocent girls not only with no money but with "No Name." To make matters worse, the money goes to Vanstone's elderly brother, who has nourished an unjust but bitter grievance against Vanstone and utterly refuses to share the inheritance with the two daughters. Norah accepts her fate passively but Magdalen sets out to seek not only vengeance but restitution.

The character of Magdalen, surpassing even Marian Halcombe in resourcefulness, dominates the novel. In the opening chapters she is an eighteen-year-old beauty, her father's darling, the vivacious "star" of the amateur theatricals of the country-house set, in love with a weak but charming young man—in short, a Victorian heroine with only minor distinguishing marks. Collins carefully places her in these scenes of domestic felicity the better to contrast what she becomes after the overwhelming shock of losing her parents and her fortune. A study in obsession, Magdalen sets forth alone, taking up with sleazy characters, using her dramatic talents to earn money through stage readings, adopting disguises and false names, and generally throwing propriety to the winds in her relentless passion for justice.

Magdalen's first plan—to go on the stage—is modified when she is taken under the wing of Captain Wragge, a smalltime swindler who regards her as his "niece" through a distant relationship. Wragge, a character straight out of

Dickens with his one brown and one green eye and his jaunty roguishness, prepares Magdalen to do dramatic stage readings at which her charm and real acting talent make her a financial success. For his part of the bargain, Wragge becomes her ally in plotting revenge against her uncle. The suspense in the novel is generated through a series of attempts on Magdalen's part to regain her fortune, each time frustrated and each time leading to another elaborate plot. When the uncle dies, she and Wragge concentrate upon the sickly young man who is his heir and find a worthy opponent in the scheming housekeeper, Mrs. Lecount, a marvelous creation with her demure manner and her implacable greed. As he did in *The Woman in White*, Collins keeps the events moving briskly, alternating Magdalen's hope and despair in her quest for revenge.

Magdalen Vanstone is the most powerful woman character Collins had yet created. Like Becky Sharpe, she takes her fate into her own hands, but unlike her prototype in *Vanity Fair* Magdalen is presented as a virtuous heroine. Fascinating as Becky was, Thackeray himself was never in doubt that she belonged on the nether side of that delicate line between bad and good, whereas in *No Name* Collins makes a case for his heroine as being faulty but forgiveable. Not so the more prudish Victorian reviewers, who pounced upon Magdalen, accusing her of "unscrupulous selfishness" and of pursuing a "career of vulgar and aimless trickery and wickedness, with which it is impossible to have a shadow of sympathy."[27] When Collins gave Magdalen the traditional "happy ending," he was not merely catering to popular taste but was clearly defending her against the moral stigma assigned to her by the Grundyites. In his preface Collins makes this explicit: "Here is one more book that depicts the struggle of a human creature, under those opposing influences of Good and Evil, which we have all felt, which we have all known. It has been my aim to make the character of 'Magdalen,' which personifies struggle, a pathetic character even in its perversity and error . . . by a resolute adherence throughout to the truth as it is in Nature." He wants society to acknowledge that Magdalen should be admired, not condemned.

By the decade of the 1860s, Collins's years of apprenticeship as a writer had come to fruition, as Dickens noted in a glowing letter to Collins of September 20, 1862 after reading *No Name:* "I have gone through the Second Volume at a setting, and I find it *wonderfully fine*. It goes on with an ever-rising power and force in it that fills me with admiration. . . . I cannot tell you with what a strange dash of pride as well as pleasure I read the great results of your hard work. Because, as you know, I was certain from the *Basil* days that you were the Writer who would come ahead of all the Field."

Equally fine is Collins's next novel, *Armadale*, which ran in *The Cornhill Magazine* from November 1864 to June 1866. T. S. Eliot placed it high in the rank of Collins's novels, praising it especially for having, like all Collins's work, "the merit of never being dull."[28]

Taking a new direction in Collins's fiction, *Armadale* is

less a mystery story than a novel dominated by the forces of destiny. Two young men named Allan Armadale—one fair, the other dark—are the sons of fathers who had been mortal enemies. One father had murdered the other in revenge for a deception which robbed him of his fortune and his fiancée. The mother of the fair Allan lives in terror that the vendetta will recur in the second generation. Ironically, her son meets the dark Allan, who has taken the name of Ozias Midwinter, and the two become devoted friends. Collins skirts very close to the supernatural in this novel, as the fair Allan has a dream in which three ominous scenes forebode danger. Although the elements causing the dream are logically accounted for, the events of the dream begin to appear in Allan's life, creating a spine-tingling sense of impending doom. The fatality which haunts the lives of the two Allans is ingeniously developed in the novel.

Again, as in *No Name*, a strong woman is the central character in *Armadale*. While the characters of the two Allans are interestingly contrasted—the fair Allan friendly, impulsive, but weak, and the dark "Ozias Midwinter" a brooding Heathcliff, bitter about his vagabond childhood but strengthened through adversity—the character of Lydia Gwilt dominates the story. Collins once remarked that novelists should have female villains as well as male ones and in Miss Gwilt he produced a superb example of the type. Her beauty is dazzling: luxuriant red hair, broad forehead, large eyes of "purely blue colour," and "the lovely complexion which accompanies such hair as hers—so delicately bright in its rosier tint, so warmly and softly white in its gentler gradations of colour on the forehead and neck." She walks with the "easy, seductive grace" which is a hallmark of all Collins's beautiful women and speaks with a charm and modesty that totally belie her scheming nature. Unlike Magdalen Vanstone in *No Name*, who remains on the side of virtue, Lydia Gwilt is truly evil—a Keatsian *belle dame*, a seductress who will stop at nothing, not even murder, to gain her ends. In a successful adaptation for the stage, the title of the novel was changed to *Miss Gwilt* and offered a plum role for the leading lady.

By the time *Armadale* appeared in the mid-1860s, many English critics had begun to use the term "sensation novels" as a pejorative label for fiction that seemed to seek excitement at the expense of a more serious presentation of life. Wilkie Collins was generally granted the dubious honor of leader of the sensation school and was often admonished for not addressing his considerable talents to higher things, especially if no moral lesson was implied in his fiction. As one reviewer of *Armadale* declared, writers like Dickens might be forgiven the use of sensational events so long as they adhered to the principle "not to show a horror without a suggestion towards its cure." Describing *Armadale* as a "'sensation novel' with a vengeance," the reviewer is especially incensed at Collins's failure to express moral condemnation of the character of Lydia Gwilt, whom he calls "one of the most hardened female villains whose devices and desires ever blackened fiction."[29] This very flouting of convention, of what Collins in one of his provocative prefaces called "the Clap-trap morality of the present day," may have enraged some of his prudish contemporaries but delighted the general body of his readers, who bought his works in ever-increasing numbers.

Although *Armadale* is essentially a novel of suspense rather than detection, a few details are suggestive of future detective fiction. There is a coarse and greedy "Confidential Spy" who anticipates the seedy characters of the hard-boiled school of the 1930s. There is some good amateur detection by the young lawyer, Pedgrift, Jr., who astonishes Allan by going to the cabstand in Bayswater and tracing the cabman who had taken a fare to Pimlico, a device that was to become a staple for Sherlock Holmes. There is the trick used by Pedgrift's father to elicit information from his clients. In a device since immortalized by Sergeant Columbo of television fame, and known in the novel as "Pedgrift's Postscript," he gives the person to be questioned a false sense of security by saying farewell and walking away, only to return abruptly to ask a crucial question, catching his victim off guard. Finally, there is Collins's use of the elaborate apparatus for murder by poison gas which forecasts the scientific gadgetry so popular in twentieth-century mystery fiction.

THE MOONSTONE

When *The Moonstone* began its run in *All the Year Round* in 1868 the magazine's sales soared as they had done during the publication of *The Woman in White*. As the closing chapters of the story appeared, crowds again gathered outside the office to get their copies of the latest installment. Even Dickens's popularity had never matched the wild enthusiasm of the readers awaiting the answer to what had happened to Rachel Verinder's diamond. Here again was a superb novel with lively characters, in which the central focus of the plot was the solving of a puzzle, enhanced in *The Moonstone* by an eccentric detective figure in Sergeant Cuff. Dorothy L. Sayers has paid the novel the ultimate tribute when she calls *The Moonstone* "probably the very finest detective story ever written. By comparison with its wide scope, its dove-tailed completeness and the marvellous variety and soundness of its characterization, modern mystery fiction looks thin and mechanical. Nothing human is perfect, but *The Moonstone* comes about as near perfection as anything of its kind can be."[30]

A significant innovation in *The Moonstone* is Collins's use of the whodunit formula. In *The Woman in White* the villains were known: all the questions began with "how?" How did Count Fosco and Sir Percival do what they did? How can it be proved? How can justice be obtained? *The Moonstone* sets the pattern for the question "who?" by placing a group of suspects in an isolated setting, each of whom may have motive or opportunity to commit the crime.

When Rachel Verinder, on her eighteenth birthday, receives a legacy of an enormous diamond, she regards as mere fantasy the legend that the stone had been stolen from the forehead of a god in a sacred shrine in India and that it would bring a curse upon its owners. Even the appearance of three mysterious Indian jugglers at her dinner party does not alarm her. Before retiring, she places the diamond in a cabinet in the boudoir next to her bedroom, in the presence of her mother, Lady Verinder, her cousins, Franklin Blake and Godfrey Ablewhite, and several of the servants. When the diamond disappears during the course of the night, the stage is set for suspicion to fall upon one after another of the members of the household. The setting in a country house, with the servants, the gentry, and perhaps a titled aristocrat or two, became a familiar format in the classical school of mystery fiction which developed in Great Britain in the early twentieth century. Certainly fiction before Collins had contained elements of crime shrouded in mystery, but these were usually subsidiary parts of a larger narrative, as in Dickens's *Bleak House*. The originality of *The Moonstone* lies in its sustaining of suspense throughout the novel—and a lengthy novel at that—on the single question of who has taken the diamond.

In *The Moonstone* Collins again uses a series of narrators who testify to the events within their own observation. The characters are charmingly individualized, sometimes generating amusing irony through their idiosyncratic views of the scene. The old servant Gabriel Betteredge sets the tone of gentle humor with his musings on how the idle rich must find ways to fill their time, and with his finding of texts for all seasons in *Robinson Crusoe*, ironically spoofing Biblical text-finders. The character of Miss Clack, with her eternal tracts, comes closer to caricature than any other in the novel but gives a wonderfully entertaining picture of the evangelical type whose religious cant Collins so despised. Franklin Blake, with the "French, German, and Italian sides" to his character, is a lively and engaging hero.

In contrast to the generally prevailing lighthearted humor in the novel, a note of tragedy appears in the character of Ezra Jennings, one of the most complex of the narrators. A West Indian of mixed blood, he is a social outcast despite his intelligence and his competence as a doctor. During the long and painful illness from which he has suffered, he has taken opium, as Collins himself did. It is important to note that Collins, like Jennings, took the drug in order to cope with the severe pains of illness, regarding it as a benign substance, what Jennings calls "that all-potent and all-merciful drug" to which he is grateful for the respite it has given him. Collins seemed to feel none of the guilt usually associated with excessive use of the drug, since he took it not for its exhilarating effect but only from necessity. At the same time, the inevitable addiction took its toll, and there is little doubt that the debilitating effects so movingly described by Ezra Jennings in the novel were Collins's own.

Another tragic character in the novel, the servant Rosanna Spearman, is the source of some social as well as moral commentary. Because Rosanna had been rescued from a woman's reformatory by Lady Verinder, she is a prime suspect when the theft of the diamond is discovered. Surprisingly, she is treated with exemplary fairness by those who know her past. Lady Verinder defends her loyally, and Sergeant Cuff, although he recognizes her from the reformatory, does not betray her to her fellow servants. Collins's implication is that most mistresses and policemen in that society would have condemned the girl without a second thought. Rosanna's ill-fated passion for Franklin Blake is the more obsessive because as a plain servant girl she is utterly beneath his notice. Her friend Limping Lucy's cry that "the day is not far off when the poor will rise against the rich" is directed against Franklin Blake, not so much because he could logically be held responsible for Rosanna's suicide as because he seems to her a symbol of a society in which class barriers exist.

In the superb creation of Sergeant Cuff in *The Moonstone*, Collins extends the development of the fictional detective begun by Dickens in the portrait of Inspector Bucket in *Bleak House*. Like his prototype, Cuff is a splendid representative of the London Detective Police whom Dickens so much admired. Through his work with Dickens on the staff of *Household Words* in the early 1850s, Collins had met the Scotland Yard officers and shared Dickens's interest in the new force. Like Bucket, Sergeant Cuff has earned a reputation for competence. When Franklin Blake hears that Cuff is being sent from London, he is delighted, telling Gabriel that "if half the stories I have heard are true, when it comes to unravelling a mystery there isn't the equal in England of Sergeant Cuff!" (I, Ch. 12) Cuff's first inquiries into the disappearance of the diamond give him the chance to show his powers in contrast with the pompous local officer, Superintendent Seegrave, who heads a long line of inept plodders serving as foils to great detectives in literature. When Seegrave refers to the smear of paint on Rachel's door as a "trifle," he is promptly rebuked by Cuff:

> I made a private inquiry last week, Mr. Superinten-
> dent. . . . At one end of the inquiry there was a murder,
> and at the other end there was a spot of ink on a table-
> cloth that nobody could account for. In all my experience
> along the dirtiest ways of this dirty little world I have
> never met with such a thing as a trifle yet. Before we go a
> step farther in this business we must see the petticoat that
> made the smear, and we must know for certain when that
> paint was wet. (I, Ch. 12)

Cuff combines scientific methods with psychology. He examines the smeared paint with a magnifying glass to exclude its having been made by human hands; he recognizes and analyzes the importance of the time element in the drying of the paint; at the same times, he sees the damage done by Seegrave's alienation of the servants and sets about charming them into cooperation, infecting even the reluctant Gabriel with "detective fever" as he studies the laundry book or traces footsteps in the sand.

Collins often liked to use incidents from actual criminal cases in his novels. Just as the abduction of Laura in *The Woman in White* had its origin in the case of the Marquise de Douhault, so the episode of the "washing-book" in *The Moonstone* was suggested by the notorious Kent murder case, which had been widely publicized in 1861.[31] A young girl, Constance Kent, was arrested for the murder of her small brother, largely on the evidence of Inspector Whicher of the London Detective Police, who was assigned to the case. The Inspector noted that the household laundry book listed a nightgown belonging to the sister that could not be accounted for, presumably because it was bloodstained and had therefore been destroyed. Such circumstantial evidence was not sufficient to convict the girl, and Sergeant Whicher was much criticized, only to be vindicated when she later confessed to the murder.

Collins's use of the laundry-book incident in *The Moonstone* has led to the assumption that Whicher was the prototype for Sergeant Cuff. However, while their methods may be similar, in person they are quite different. Whicher (then a sergeant) appears in Dickens's article in *Household Words* in 1850 as a short and stocky man with somewhat colloquial speech, while Cuff is lean and grizzled, and his speech is considerably more genteel. Shaw's Professor Higgins would no doubt have placed Cuff a notch or two above Whicher on the social scale. Cuff's melancholy air and his love of roses, setting the pattern for the eccentricities of a host of fictional detectives, are Collins's own creations.

Unlike his successors in detective fiction, Cuff is not infallible. Although his methods are impeccable, his first solution to the mystery proves to be quite wrong. His retirement to the country to grow roses prefigures Sherlock Holmes and his bees or Hercule Poirot and his vegetable marrows, but unlike those sleuths, Cuff is not the central figure in the story. He disappears for a long segment of the novel, reappearing in the end to trace the diamond and reveal the fate of Godfrey Ablewhite. Only later did mystery writers make the detective the center of interest upon which the story depends.

In *The Moonstone* Collins again uses some of the devices for deceiving the reader with which he experimented in *The Woman in White*. Like Anne Catherick, Rosanna Spearman is the victim of "deceptive misinformation." Believing that Franklin Blake's paint-stained nightgown is proof of his guilt, Rosanna inadvertently leaves a spectacular trail of false clues in her misguided desire to shield him.

The device of "buried information" is brilliantly used in the scene on the evening of Rachel's birthday to conceal the central key to the mystery—the administration of the opium to Blake without his knowledge. What appears to be the idle and amusing chatter of the dinner guests in fact contains the argument between Mr. Candy and Franklin about the merits of the medical profession, spurring the doctor to try his experiment with the opium. Only on second reading would the reader note that Mr. Candy slips away briefly from the other guests, that he is seen laughing conspiratorially with Godfrey, and that Godfrey hands Franklin his nightcap of brandy. The "facts" are fairly laid out but have been ingeniously buried among apparently trivial incidents.

Two other devices of deception appear in *The Moonstone* and constitute important innovations in the development of mystery fiction. The first of these is "the guilt of the least likely suspect," which has become a standard part of the whodunit repertory. The reader is aware that Rachel believes Franklin to have had some part in the theft, but the assumption is that she is mistaken. A best guess might be that Godfrey stole the diamond while wearing Franklin's nightgown. When Rachel reveals that she actually saw Franklin take the diamond, the mystery is far from solved, for he "knows" that he is innocent. He thus remains the least likely suspect until the final solution is revealed.

Writers on Collins have sometimes noted his use of the least likely suspect, but none seems to have observed Collins's use in *The Moonstone* of the "ironclad alibi." Since Godfrey Ablewhite is an obvious suspect, the puzzle seems more insoluble than ever when Rachel declares that she "knows" Godfrey did not take the diamond. Miss Clack triumphantly produces Rachel's statement to Mr. Bruff, another of Collins's faithful family lawyers, in defense of her beloved Godfrey. Bruff's reply adds the weight of his authority to Rachel's belief: "If Rachel has testified to his innocence, Miss Clack, I don't scruple to say that I believe in his innocence as firmly as you do. I have been misled by appearances, like the rest of the world." Since Rachel's truthfulness is one of the verities on which the entire plot hinges, Godfrey has been given an ironclad alibi, which the reader, like Mr. Bruff, accepts.

The Moonstone is an altogether delightful work. Most of the events of the story take place in a sunlit world of everyday reality. Even the wonderfully haunting scenes at the Shivering Sand are part of the realistic life of the country house and the fishermen's village. Yet hovering over this picture of mid-Victorian English life is the exotic story of the Indian diamond and its violent history. The novel closes with the memorable picture of the shrine in a wild and remote region of India, observed by the traveler Mr. Murthwaite:

> There, raised high on a throne, seated on his typical antelope, with his four arms stretching toward the four corners of the earth, there soared above us, dark and awful in the mystic light of heaven, the god of the Moon. And there, in the forehead of the deity, gleamed the yellow Diamond, whose splendor had last shone on me in England, from the bosom of a woman's dress.

LAST WORKS

When Wilkie Collins turned away from the formula of *The Moonstone*, which had brought him such success, and began to write novels of social protest, the quality of his fiction sharply declined. From 1870 until his death in 1889 Collins addressed himself in his novels to attacks upon such varied topics as the marriage laws of Scotland, athleticism, society's intolerance of fallen women, vivisection and scientific research, the treatment of the insane, the Roman Catholic Church, and theories of heredity. The poet Swinburne offered a couplet to note the falling off of Collins's work as he became "teacher and preacher":

> What brought good Wilkie's genius nigh perdition?
> Some demon whispered—"Wilkie! have a mission."[32]

While it is true that Collins's talents were less disposed

than those of writers like Dickens or Charles Reade to the successful blending of social protest with the telling of a story, it seems probable that the cause of his decline lies elsewhere than in the mere change of purpose in his fiction. Within two years after the appearance of *The Moonstone* the whole atmosphere of his novels exhibits a dramatic change. Unlike the genial and often witty observations of human nature that characterized the teller of the earlier fiction, the author's tone in the late novels is often strident and sometimes more vitriolic than the subject under attack seems to warrant. Furthermore, the fiction is marred by excessive improbabilities and by characters whose behavior is dubiously motivated. Such a change argues a physical and perhaps emotional deterioration which could well be caused by his more and more frequent bouts of illness and the consequent increase in his opium addiction.

Whatever the cause of his decline, Collins never entirely lost his talent for telling a good story. A group of short tales from the 1870s and 1880s collected under the title "Little Novels," are in a lighter vein than the late novels and afford some entertainment, although they are generally inferior to the short stories of the 1850s.

A few of Collins's late works contain elements of mystery and suspense which deserve recognition. The novelette *My Lady's Money* (1879) is a pleasant little whodunit of theft, with an eccentric detective figure, a disbarred solicitor called Old Sharon, probably intended to resemble Gaboriau's Père Tabaret. In contrast to the austere and clerical-looking Sergeant Cuff, Old Sharon is a "small, fat, bald-headed, dirty, old man," disreputable but shrewd. After hearing the facts in the case, literally in his arm-chair, he announces that he knows who is guilty but will have to go forth to gather proof. The story ends with a nice twist, as the reader is led toward a false solution, while Old Sharon triumphantly produces the correct one.

Perhaps the best of the late novels is *The Law and the Lady* (1875) in which the inevitable protest, this time against the Scottish verdict of "not proven" in criminal trials, is woven successfully into a genuine murder mystery, complete with a group of suspects and a surprise solution.

Valeria Macallan, a strong and attractive heroine reminiscent of Magdalen Vanstone, sets out to prove her husband innocent of the murder of his first wife and to erase what he regards as the ineradicable stain of the Scottish jury's verdict of "not proven" in his murder trial. In Scotland at that time the jury had the option of bringing in such a verdict if they believed the evidence was insufficient to convict. Although the accused was free to go, there was a strong presumption in the public mind that the jury had believed him to be guilty. In *The Law and the Lady* the weak-willed Eustace Macallan seems scarcely worthy of his wife's devotion, as she refuses to give up against all odds. She visits his country estate where the first wife had died, reconstructing the circumstances surrounding the death. Collins again develops the formula of a group of characters, each with a motive, and each falling under suspicion. The story is seriously marred by the introduction of the grotesque figure of Misserimus Dexter, a legless cripple who ultimately goes mad. With this exception, the plot is worked out with something of Collins's earlier ingenuity and provides a good example of a successful mystery format in his late fiction.

In the works of Wilkie Collins, we have seen how the elements of the social and the "sensational" in fiction, along with Collins's genius for creating a suspenseful plot, came together to produce the mystery novel. After the publication of *The Woman in White*, a host of imitators appeared, and after *The Moonstone* Collins was recognized as the master of the new literary form.

3

Dickens and Detection

The fictional world of Charles Dickens covers so broad a spectrum that he has been viewed in as many guises as there are critics and readers to scan him. For some he is the consummate humorist, the inventor of lovable Mr. Pickwick, the inimitable Sam Weller, and a host of their descendants from Mr. Micawber to Pecksniff. To others, especially to his contemporaries, he was also the master of sentimentality, evoking smiles and tears with heart-tugging delicacy in episodes of love or death. To Victorian readers great death scenes were as essential for popular success as scenes of sex are in the 1980s, and all England—including Dickens himself—wept over the deaths of Little Nell and Paul Dombey. To some, Dickens was an exploiter of the popular taste for crime and violence, a "sensation novelist" par excellence, vulgarly appealing to the lowest audience through his method of publishing in cheap serial form before bringing out the hardcover volumes of his novels. Finally, he was seen as the great social critic—the English Balzac—who used his fiction brilliantly in order to expose the evils of the social system and to imply the need for reform.

Of course Dickens was all of these things and more. Among twentieth-century literary critics he has been psychoanalyzed by the Freudians, appraised by the Marxists, combed for symbols, weighed and measured from every angle, all with the consensus that his genius has a magic transcending analysis.

Although Dickens was not essentially a writer of mystery or detective fiction, he made some important contributions to the genre. His interest in crime as a social problem crops up throughout his fiction, from the thieves' den in *Oliver Twist* to the opium den in *Edwin Drood*. Beginning as a skeptic of police and detection, Dickens turned into an influential champion of the London Detective Police, as reflected in the various detective figures in his fiction. He gradually showed a growing interest in the technique of suspense plotting, in which the influence of Wilkie Collins played a part. Finally, in *The Mystery of Edwin Drood*, he was moving into the realm of the full-fledged mystery novel at the time of his death.

THE LIFE

The early years of Dickens's childhood were happy ones. His father, John Dickens, was a clerk in the Naval Pay Office in Portsmouth when Charles Dickens was born at nearby Portsea on February 7, 1812, the second of what was to be a family of eight children. John Dickens's salary at this time was enough by the standards of the day for the family to live in modest comfort, and by 1817, when they moved to Chatham, near Rochester, his income had more than doubled.[1] At Chatham the family occupied a pleasant house in an affluent neighborhood, with two servants and other accoutrements of gentility. Such social distinctions were especially important to John Dickens's efforts to rise above the social level of his parents, who were upper servants in the household of the Marquess of Blandford. Had he been able to live within his income, his success would have been assured, but like Mr. Micawber, he kept the family in constant debt through his lavish spending.

Young Charles was small for his age and not robust enough for boys' games but was an apt pupil at school. From an early age he had shown the talent for songs and mimicry which forecast his lifelong delight in theatrical performance. He adored his genial father, who took him on long walks in the cathedral town of Rochester and the surrounding countryside. When Charles especially admired the house on nearby Gad's Hill, his father, never loath to build castles in the air, assured him that with proper industry he might live there one day. Dickens always remembered these golden years of childhood at Rochester as a kind of Eden, which made the subsequent fall into poverty all the more painful to the sensitive boy. The crash came in 1823 when the elder Dickens's debts forced a move to London, where the ever-increasing family lived precariously, pawning one after another of their possessions in a desperate attempt to survive. It was here that Charles, not yet twelve years old, was put to work in a blacking factory in the Strand, wrapping and labeling bottles in the company of rough, uncouth boys from the slums of London.

Soon thereafter, when certain creditors refused to extend their bills, John Dickens was imprisoned in the Marshalsea for debt. At that time, debtors might bring their families to live in the prison, from which all but the debtor could come and go freely. Prisoners paid according to their means for rooms, food, and other services. Those with no money at all were housed in the "hole," where they might starve except for whatever they could beg at the prison gates. As an employee of the Navy Pay office, John Dickens still received a subsistence, to which were added the few shillings each week from Charles's wages at the warehouse. Thus the family lived decently enough. Because the prison was too far from his work, Charles was lodged outside and visited only on the weekends, feeling bitterly not only the disgrace of their imprisonment but also his exclusion from the family circle.

At the end of three months, John Dickens received a legacy through the death of his mother, the housekeeper at Crewe who later appeared as Mrs. Rouncewell in *Bleak House*. The creditors were paid and the family left the prison, but no one seemed to consider relieving Charles of his job in the blacking factory. For another three months he toiled on, loathing the surroundings, suffering from attacks of illness, and feeling emotionally abandoned by his parents. At last his father rescued him from his drudgery and sent him to school, where he delighted in learning and became a prize pupil.

The whole episode of the prison and the factory was so

devastating to his pride that Dickens never spoke of it to anyone. His wife, children, and friends did not know until after his death that little David Copperfield's experience in the warehouse was Dickens's own. In an autobiographical statement given to John Forster, his future biographer, Dickens wrote: "No words can express the secret agony of my soul . . . as I felt my early hopes of growing up to be a learned and distinguished man crushed in my breast. The deep remembrance of the sense I had of being utterly neglected and hopeless; of the shame I felt in my position; of the misery it was to my young heart to believe that, day by day, what I had learned and thought, and delighted in . . . was passing away from me, never to be brought back any more, cannot be written."[2] The experience, brief though it was, awakened in the sensitive boy an abhorrence of poverty and a lifelong dedication to alleviating the plight of its victims.

When he was fifteen, Charles left school and became an office boy for a firm of solicitors, where he first formed his opinion of the law as cumbersome and inefficient. Too impatient to study law and read for the bar, Dickens always retained his layman's view of its delays without grasping the larger principles of justice that distinguish the English law from other systems, despite its shortcomings. Following the lead of his father, who was then working as a journalist, Dickens taught himself shorthand, working by the age of seventeen as a free-lance court reporter, both in Doctors' Commons and in the Metropolitan Police Courts. Two years later he began reporting Parliamentary debates for his uncle's paper, *The Mirror of Parliament*, where he was renowned for the speed and accuracy of his shorthand and transcription. Early in 1832 he joined the staff of the new evening daily, the *True Sun,* doing general as well as Parliamentary reporting. This was the period of the dramatic debates on the Reform Bill, which finally passed in that year, greatly extending the franchise and reapportioning representation in the House of Commons. While Dickens approved of the political reform thus achieved, his daily attendance at sessions of Parliament gave him an unflattering opinion of politicians, most of whom he regarded as pompous and self-serving.

During these years as a reporter Dickens had fallen passionately in love with a banker's daughter named Maria Beadnell, whose coquettish charms enchanted and tortured him by turns. Despite his lack of sufficient income to qualify to Mr. Beadnell as a serious suitor, and despite Maria's obvious uncertainty as to whether or not she loved him, Dickens threw himself into his pursuit of her with all the obsession that characterized his approach to any goal throughout his life. He had no illusions about Maria's character; he knew that she was childish, unreliable, and vacillating; he quite simply loved her to distraction. When he was at last forced to give up the real Maria, he later presented her vicariously to David Copperfield as Dora and gave the world an unforgettable picture of youthful infatuation.

In 1834 Dickens began to write sketches, which were at first published anonymously and then signed "Boz," after his small brother who had been called "Moses," pronounced nasally as "Bozes," and shortened to "Boz." By

1836, when the collected *Sketches by Boz* sold briskly, Dickens knew that writing was to be his career. *Pickwick Papers* followed with spectacular success, and such was Dickens's energy that by 1838 he was working simultaneously on *Oliver Twist* and *Nicholas Nickleby*, turning out installments just ahead of the printer, and at the same time editing *Bentley's Miscellany* and writing short pieces for the magazines. He soon became the most popular writer of the day, earning sums of money that would have dazzled the small boy in the blacking factory.

Meanwhile, at the first sign of financial success in 1836, Dickens had married Catherine Hogarth, the daughter of a newspaper colleague. Although fond enough of Catherine in the beginning, he felt for her none of the fine madness of his passion for Maria Beadnell. Catherine was mildly pretty and placid but never a match for the dynamic Dickens. She gave birth to ten children, nine of whom survived, and Dickens threw himself with his usual enthusiasm into organizing family games and excursions while still vigorously pursuing his writing.

After the success of *The Old Curiosity Shop* and *Barnaby Rudge*, Dickens made a triumphant tour of the United States in 1842, where he was lionized from Boston to St. Louis, from Richmond to Cincinnati. In Philadelphia he met an unknown young writer named Edgar Allan Poe, whose work he admired. Although professing pleasure in the friendliness of the American people, Dickens soon wearied of the vulgarity of manners in what was still, outside the Eastern cities, a frontier society. In the following year, when the sales of *Martin Chuzzlewit* fell off, he had Martin go off to America, where the scathing account of his experience there reflected Dickens's own repugnance.

Dickens was a man of boundless energy who loved entertaining and being surrounded by his friends. A born actor, he reveled in producing amateur theatricals for charitable causes, sometimes taking his troupe of friends and family members on tours through the provinces. In addition to his favorite companion, Wilkie Collins, his immediate circle included the novelist Edward Bulwer Lytton, the biographer John Forster, artists Augustus Egg and Daniel Maclise, his editor John Wills, the actor William Macready, and others. His friendships also included such famed contemporaries as Tennyson, Browning, Thackeray, and Trollope.

London was always for Dickens the center for his creative imagination. He walked its streets at night, explored the squalor of its slums, visited its dens of crime, reveled in its theaters, and generally yearned for its familiar surroundings when he was away from it for long. Although the family spent many weeks of each year at Broadstairs and other seaside towns, and often lived abroad for months at a time, Dickens's fictional characters are for the most part products of the metropolis.

His observations of London poverty and crime fired his zeal for the reform of social evils wherever they might occur. Each novel, in addition to its marvelous cast of eccentrics and its passages of incomparable comedy, exposes a social problem of one kind or another: in *Oliver Twist* the plight of children born in the workhouse and victimized by gangs of thieves, in *Nicholas Nickleby* the appalling conditions in boarding schools where boys were beaten and starved, in *The Old Curiosity Shop* more glimpses of London crime, in *Dombey and Son* the greed of the coldhearted businessman, and in *David Copperfield*, as already noted, the conditions of child labor in the blacking factory.

The novels of the 1850s continue the pattern. *Bleak House* attacks the delays of the law; *Hard Times* moves to the midlands to deal with working conditions in the mills; *Little Dorrit* attacks government bureaucracy in the "Circumlocution Office" and describes the conditions in the Marshalsea prison, but with never a word to disclose Dickens's own family's experience there; *A Tale of Two Cities* explores the grievances that led to the French Revolution but also condemns the violence that ensued.

The decade of the 1850s brought dramatic changes in Dickens's life. In 1850 he launched his own magazine, *Household Words*, which proved to be successful. In 1855 he learned by chance that the house at Gad's Hill near Rochester, which he had admired as a child, was for sale, and was delighted to fulfill his childhood fantasy by acquiring the charming house with its spacious grounds. Although he continued to maintain a place in London, the house at Gad's Hill, only thirty miles away, became the center of his life. In 1858 he began the series of public readings that consumed his energies and ultimately destroyed his health; and in the same year occurred his fateful meeting with Ellen Ternan, the young actress with whom he fell in love. Despite the inevitable scandal, he effected a permanent separation from Catherine, giving her a house in London while he retained Gad's Hill. The relationship with Ellen did not bring Dickens the happiness he longed for. She apparently did not return his affection and succumbed to him with some reluctance, in order to obtain financial security for herself and for her mother and sisters.[3]

The theme of unrequited love, echoing Dickens's anguish over Ellen Ternan, is reflected in his last three novels. In *Great Expectations* (1860) Pip adores Estella despite her cruelty to him; in *Our Mutual Friend* (1865) Bradley Headstone is obsessed to the point of madness by his hopeless passion for Lizzie Hexham; and in the unfinished *The Mystery of Edwin Drood* (1870) John Jasper is tortured by his fruitless worship of little Rosa Bud.

Dickens's public readings, begun in 1858, proved to be not only profitable but addictive. He was a superb actor, with a natural gift for holding his audience in the palm of his hand, and the readings were enormously popular. Whatever the frustrations of his personal life, those hours in the theater with the audience weeping over Tiny Tim or Little Nell, chuckling over Sam Weller or Mrs. Gamp, or prostrated (sometimes literally) over Sykes's murder of Nancy, became the high points of his existence. As his health began to fail, his physical exhaustion at the end of each reading became alarming, yet he could not take the advice of family and friends to give up and rest. What he had written to Forster earlier remained true to the end:

> Too late to say, put the curb on, and don't rush at hills— the wrong man to say it to. I have now no relief but in

action. I am become incapable of rest. I am quite confident
I should rust, break, and die, if I spared myself. Much
better to die, doing. What I am in that way, nature made
me.[4]

On June 6, 1870, he was at Gad's Hill working on
the current installment of *Edwin Drood* when he suffered a
paralytic stroke and died two days later. The dynamic energy that had driven him throughout his life had failed at
last, but in his own words to Forster, he had died as he
would have wished, "while doing."

MYSTERY PLOTS AND DETECTIVES

Dickens never held a high opinion of the Bow Street Runners. Perhaps his childhood exposure to poverty, combined with his family's desperate effort to cling to the
fringes of the middle class, left him with a deep commitment to a society that observed moral standards. Much as
he despised and satirized the evangelical hypocrisy of the
Chadbands of this world, he nevertheless upheld throughout his fiction the principles of virtue and goodness; evil
deeds must be exposed and punished and the moral order
restored before each novel could reach a satisfactory conclusion. Repelled by the occasional scandals that had
tainted the reputation of the Runners, Dickens seemed to
doubt not only their integrity but their efficiency as well.

In 1838, the year before the Runners were officially
disbanded, he introduced a pair of Runners into *Oliver
Twist*, which was coming out in serial form in that year.
When Sykes and his crew use little Oliver in the robbery

of the Maylie house, Blathers and Duff are sent out from Bow Street to investigate. As their Dickensian tag names imply, the two officers are little short of buffoons in the Shakespearean tradition of Dogberry and Verges. "Now, what is this, about this here boy that the servants are a-talking on?" asks Blathers. When Doctor Losberne assures them that it is nothing, a mere mistake of one of the servants, Duff remarks: "Wery easy disposed of, if it is" (Ch. 29). Such bumblers are easily duped into believing that Oliver was not involved in the robbery. Not for Dickens was the romantic view of the Runners which some writers had made popular.

Dickens's interest in crime and its detection can be seen in his fiction not only through his changing attitudes toward the police but also in his experiments with mystery plots. *Barnaby Rudge* (1841) begins with what appears to be a proper murder mystery, but it soon becomes apparent that Dickens's heart is not in the development of his plot. The novel opens with the locals gathered round the inn fire recounting the oft-told tale of the murder, some twenty years before, of Reuben Haredale, the local squire, while a mysterious stranger listens from a darkened corner. Only Haredale's steward and gardener had been on the premises on the night of the murder, and when some months later a body had been found in an abandoned quarry, it was unrecognizable except for the clothing, which was identified as that of the steward Rudge. The missing gardener was therefore assumed to be the murderer of both Haredale and Rudge.

Edgar Allan Poe, reading the early installments of the

novel in America, is reported to have predicted at once that it was Rudge who was the guilty man, having killed the gardener and dressed the body in Rudge's clothing.[5] Modern mystery buffs, after more than a century of elaborate plots, would spot this probability with ease, but Dickens's readers, fresh to the plot and lacking Poe's ratiocinative powers, might have been readily deceived had Dickens made a real effort to conceal the truth. However, by the fifth chapter, when Mrs. Rudge is shown to be in great fear of the mysterious stranger yet desperately protecting him from exposure, even the most naive reader could see that he was the missing Rudge. Apparently Dickens felt that sustaining the suspense was not worth the effort, for his chief interest in the novel lay in depicting the events of the Gordon Riots of 1780. His theme in *Barnaby Rudge*—as in *A Tale of Two cities*, his only other venture into historical fiction—is that mob violence is always to be deplored, whatever the apparent justice of its original cause. The murder mystery is almost forgotten through long segments of the novel and bears only a tenuous connection with the historical scenes. In the end, a certain amount of detective work is done by the murdered man's brother, who follows up some rather obvious clues to Rudge as the murderer. Like Wilkie Collins's early attempts at suspense in *Hide and Seek* (1854) and *The Dead Secret* (1857), Dickens's mystery plot was too transparent; but whereas Collins, a decade later, was trying to make the mystery the central focus of the total novel, Dickens's emphasis was still very much on social concerns.

Murder figures again in *Martin Chuzzlewit* (1844), but

not with an element of suspense about who is guilty. There is a surprise twist in the revelation that Jonas Chuzzlewit had not, in fact, murdered his father, although he intended to bring about his death and believed that he had done so. When he does murder Montague Tigg, the reader is aware of his guilt, and the chief interest occurs in his exposure through the activities of the detective Nadgett.

Although a more favorable public image of the detective was emerging at this period, as noted above in Chapter 1, it was not until Dickens's personal acquaintance with the new detective police officers in 1850 that he was converted to their cause. The character of Nadgett indicates that in 1844 Dickens still shared with a large segment of the public the view that detectives, whether private or official, were often little better than paid spies and informers. In *Martin Chuzzlewit*, Nadgett, the private detective hired by Tigg to spy upon Jonas, is competent in his work but is a thoroughly unsavory creature. "He was a short, dried-up, withered old man, who seemed to have secreted his very blood; for nobody would have given him credit for the possession of six ounces of it in his whole body" (Ch. 27).

Nadgett is a typical denizen of that London underworld which so fascinated Dickens. He has no moral code beyond doing his job. He works for Tigg's obviously fraudulent Anglo-Bengalee Disinterested Loan and Life Assurance Company, intent only upon his spying, his eyes apparently on the ground but missing nothing. Nadgett's technique is ingenious: "The secret manner of the man

disarmed suspicion in this wise; suggesting, not that he
was watching any one, but that he thought some other
man was watching him. He went about so stealthily, and
kept himself so wrapped up in himself, that the whole
object of his life appeared to be, to avoid notice and preserve his own mystery" (Ch. 38). The success of this
method prepares the way for a dramatic revelation later
on, for Jonas is totally unaware that he is being watched:

> Jonas sometimes saw him in the street, hovering in the
> outer office, waiting at the door for the man who never
> came, or slinking off with his immovable face and droop-
> ing head, and the one beaver glove dangling before him;
> but he would as soon have thought of the cross upon the
> top of St. Paul's Cathedral taking note of what he did, or
> slowly winding a net about his feet, as of Nadgett's being
> engaged in such an occupation. (Ch. 38).

Although Nadgett's "immovable face" suggests that he
has no emotion, he does derive satisfaction from a job well
done, and behind the mask there is more than a hint of
contempt for the master who hires him. When he presents
"Tigg Montague" the series of notes written on backs of
old letters or scraps of paper testifying to Jonas's apparent
murder of his father, he doles out the scraps one by one,
watching as Tigg's irritation with his spy gradually
changes to "grave and serious attention":

> At first, Mr. Nadgett sat with his spectacles low down
> upon his nose, looking over them at his employer, and
> nervously rubbing his hands. After a little while, he

changed his posture in his chair for one of greater ease, and leisurely perused the next document he held ready, as if an occasional glance at his employer's face were now enough, and all occasion for anxiety and doubt were gone. And finally he rose and looked out of the window, where he stood with a triumphant air, until Tigg Montague had finished. (Ch. 38)

Unpleasant though he is, Nadgett takes pride in his work. When Tigg exclaims that he is a "good hand at a secret," Nadgett replies that nothing interests him unless it *is* a secret. In fact, he adds, "It almost takes away any pleasure I may have had in this inquiry even to make it known to you."

Nadgett's final triumph occurs in the dramatic scene in which he points out Jonas as the murderer of Montague Tigg.[6] Unlike the modern detective hero, however, he is not the center of admiration but is unceremoniously referred to as "the informer." While Dickens is clearly on the side of law and order, he presents Nadgett as a paid spy useful for catching criminals but not a fit subject for adulation. In the same scene he compounds his denigration of the police function by introducing the Chuzzlewit cousin, Chevy Slyme, in the character of a police officer whose duty it now is to arrest Jonas. Slyme's tag name expresses the social stigma attached to his occupation, and he confirms this by asking his relatives if they can see a member of their family dressed as a policeman without being embarrassed. "I took up this trade," he declares, "on purpose to shame you, but I didn't think I should have to make a capture in the family" (Ch. 51).

Dickens's change of heart about detectives first appears in 1850 in the series of articles in *Household Words* that gave such enormous impetus to public acceptance of the London Police. He begins with a contrast between the old system and the new, casting the Bow Street Runners into oblivion all the better to enhance his picture of the new Detective Force:

> We are not by any means believers in the old Bow Street Police. To say the truth, we think there was a vast amount of humbug about those worthies. Apart from many of them being men of very indifferent character, and far too much in the habit of consorting with thieves and the like, they never lost a public occasion of jobbing and trading in mystery and making the most of themselves.[7]

Ignoring the fact that some members of the new police were themselves former Runners, Dickens launches into praise of the new system:

> On the other hand, the Detective Force organized since the establishment of the existing Police, is so well chosen and trained, proceeds so systematically and quietly, does its business in such a workmanlike manner, and is always so calmly and steadily engaged in the service of the public, that the public really do not know enough of it, to know a tithe of its usefulness.[8]

Dickens then gives his readers an account of a gathering which he hosted at the offices of *Household Words* to interview the officers of the Detective Force, consisting at that time of eight members, all but one of whom were present on this occasion. The two inspectors and five sergeants are given transparently fictitious names: Inspector Field becomes "Wield," Sergeant Whicher (who later became identified as a source for Sergeant Cuff in Wilkie Collins's *the Moonstone*) is called "Witchem," Walker is "Stalker," and so on.

Dickens describes the officers in glowing terms: "They are, one and all, respectable-looking men; of perfectly good deportment and unusual intelligence; with nothing lounging or slinking in their manners; with an air of keen observation and quick perception when addressed."[9] Each officer gives an anecdote to illustrate his activities. Sergeant "Witchem" tells how he tracked down Tally-Ho Thompson of the "swell mob" by following a series of letters to their destinations. A young sergeant recounts breaking a robbery ring by posing as a naive butcher from the country. In these and in the "Three Detective Anecdotes" of the following article, the episodes illustrate not so much the brilliance of their detection as the adventurous and sometimes amusing nature of their police work and the shrewd knowledge of the criminal underworld shared by the officers. With characteristic rhetoric, Dickens emphasizes their efficiency and their dedication: "For ever on the watch, with their wits stretched to the utmost, these officers have, from day to day and year to year, to set themselves against every novelty of trickery and dexterity that the combined imaginations of all the lawless rascals in England can devise, and to keep pace with every such invention that comes out."[10]

Dickens was especially friendly with Inspector Charles Frederick Field, who took him on nocturnal visits through London's dens of vice and poverty and who became the model for Inspector Bucket in *Bleak House*. Like Bucket, Field is described as middle-aged and portly, with a "large, moist, knowing eye, a husky voice, and a habit of emphasizing his conversation by the aid of a corpulent fore-finger." In a later article entitled "On Duty with Inspector Field," Dickens accompanies the inspector on his nightly rounds. As thoroughly as Dickens already knew the appalling conditions of some areas of the city, Field could show him scenes which he could not have visited without protection. The theme that emerges most powerfully from this article is not merely the exaltation of Inspector Field himself but the affirmation that a reliable police system provides some hope for the control of crime in the city. Dickens notes that Inspector Field (now given his own name in this article) is both feared and respected by the underworld figures, as described in the visit to "Rat's Castle":

> Inspector Field's eye is the roving eye that searches every corner of the cellar as he talks. Inspector Field's hand is the well-known hand that has collared half the people here, and motioned their brothers, sisters, fathers, mothers, male and female friends, inexorably to New South Wales. Yet Inspector Field stands in this den, the Sultan of the place. Every thief here cowers before him, like a schoolboy before his schoolmaster. All watch him, all an-

swer when addressed, all laugh at his jokes, all seek to propitiate him.[11]

Most important, the thieves will come to know that they must eventually be stopped by what Dickens calls this "organized and steady system."

It is somewhat surprising, as Philip Collins points out in his *Dickens and Crime*, to find Dickens praising public officials in this "vein of boyish hero-worship."[12] We usually find him on the attack against everything official from beadles to the Circumlocution Office. His unbounded admiration for the Detective Police may have arisen from his habit of exaggeration; never one to be lukewarm in his judgments, he may simply have been indulging in his usual hyperbolic rhetoric. He was no doubt also attracted by the theatrical aspects of detection, with its frequent use of disguises and impersonations. But above all, as the article on Inspector Field testifies, Dickens warmly supported the "organized and steady system" that he believed would bring increasing order and moral stability to society.

Dickens's new admiration for detection promptly appeared in *Bleak House* (1852), where he provides Inspector Bucket with a nicely plotted murder case to solve. The mystery plot comprises only a small portion of this great novel of social satire. The legal profession is the principal target, as the case of Jarndyce vs. Jarndyce drags endlessly through the Chancery Court until the costs consume the estate. Some marvelously satiric portraits ornament the novel, from the irresponsible Harold Skimpole to Mr.

Turveydrop and his "deportment," from the greedy money-lender Smallweed to Mrs. Jellyby, devoting herself to foreign causes while neglecting her family. Within the huge design of *Bleak House*, the murder of the lawyer Tulkinghorn underscores the symbolic nature of the novel's attack upon the law. Since many people may have wished Tulkinghorn dead, Dickens creates a mini-whodunit in this portion of the novel, investing more care in sustaining suspense than he had done a decade earlier in *Barnaby Rudge*.

At first, suspicion of the murder of Tulkinghorn falls equally upon George the trooper and upon Lady Dedlock herself. George has been observed hanging about Tulkinghorn's chambers and muttering threats against the lawyer. Lady Dedlock has learned that Tulkinghorn knows the secret of her past and may reveal it at any moment to her husband. Although Dickens withholds the facts, the reader tends to believe in George's innocence because he is the kind of forthright and uncomplicated character whose trustworthiness seems beyond doubt. In the case of Lady Dedlock, however, Dickens leads the reader down the garden path with all the aplomb of the practiced mystery technician. After Tulkinghorn leaves her to return home on the night of the murder, Lady Dedlock goes out for a walk alone. Later, George remarks that he saw on the stairs on the fatal night a "shape like Miss Summerson's," wearing a deep-fringed dark shawl, an obvious reference to Lady Dedlock (Ch. 52). Finally, when Bucket is summing up his case to Sir Leicester, he first declares that the guilty party is a woman; then, after some pages of interruption sustaining the reader's suspense, he states that the woman is present in the house, seeming to confirm that she is Lady Dedlock. The arrest of the French maid, Hortense, as the real culprit, produces a surprise ending worthy of a Hercule Poirot.

Presiding over the mystery plot is the brisk but kindly figure of Inspector Bucket. Gone is the picture of the detective as an unsavory spy like Nadgett, and in its place stands the portrait of the admirable officer, dedicated to the pursuit of justice. Like his prototype, Inspector Field, Bucket is a "stoutly-built, steady-looking, sharp-eyed man in black, of about the middle-age" (Ch. 22). Like Field, he exercises his "fat forefinger" when important matters are pressing. "He puts it to his ears, and it whispers information; he puts it to his lips, and it enjoins him to secrecy; he rubs it over his nose, and it sharpens his scent; he shakes it before a guilty man, and it charms him to his destruction" (Ch. 53).

Bucket first appears in *Bleak House* when he is employed by Tulkinghorn to locate Jo, the young crossing-sweeper. When Snagsby the stationer is asked to accompany the Inspector in order to identify Jo, Bucket demonstrates his capacity for sensing people's reactions. A momentary hesitation on the part of Snagsby is promptly diagnosed by Bucket: "Don't you be afraid of hurting the boy," he says. "You won't do that" (Ch. 22). This was the reassurance that Snagsby wanted, and he goes off cheerfully with the detective.

Their journey through the London slum of Tom-all-Alone's recalls Dickens's nocturnal tours with Inspector

Field. Bucket is the indomitable officer, knowing his territory and respected by police and criminal alike: "Now and then, when they pass a police-constable on his beat, Mr. Snagsby notices that both the constable and his guide fall into a deep abstraction as they come towards each other, and to gaze into space. In a few instances, Mr. Bucket, coming behind some undersized young man with a shining hat on, and his sleek hair twisted into one flat curl on each side of his head, almost without glancing at him touches him with his stick, upon which the young man, looking round, instantly evaporates" (Ch. 22).

In this first appearance, Bucket demonstrates one of his best detective techniques, the use of shameless flattery to disarm the subject. Instead of impressing Snagsby directly with the need for silence, Bucket employs his own brand of persuasion:

> "You see, Mr. Snagsby," says Mr. Bucket, accompanying him to the door and shaking hands with him over and over again, "what I like in you is that you're a man it's of no use pumping; that's what *you* are. When you know you have done a right thing, you put it away, and it's done with and gone, and there's an end of it. That's what *you* do."
>
> "That is certainly what I endeavour to do, sir," returns Mr. Snagsby.
>
> "No, you don't do yourself justice. It an't what you endeavour to do," says Mr. Bucket, shaking hands with him and blessing him in the tenderest manner, "it's what you *do*. That's what I estimate in a man in your way of business." (Ch. 22)

Bucket exercises this technique on a number of subsequent occasions. He drops out of sight for a long segment of the novel, reappearing after Tulkinghorn's murder to take charge of the investigation. His first act is to arrest George as the chief suspect. Finding him at the home of his friends the Bagnets, Bucket ingratiates himself with the family, inventing a mythical friend who is in need of a violincello, admiring the children, confiding that he and his wife regret having no family of their own, and finally, despite the flattery, sparing George's feelings by making the arrest after they leave the Bagnets' home. Even more inventive is his treatment of the Dedlock footman from whom he elicits the information that Lady Dedlock went out alone on the night of the murder. Bucket admires the tall and handsome "Mercury," suggesting that a sculptor friend might wish to model him. He invents stories of family members who were servants, appealing to the footman as an equal who understands and admires his occupation.

Bucket's flattery extends even to Sir Leicester Dedlock himself, in a remarkable scene in which he uses precisely the same technique on the austere aristocrat that he had used on little Snagsby the stationer. Preparing Sir Leicester for learning the truth about Lady Dedlock's past, he declares that what he will hear will be a shock, but of course "a gentleman can bear a shock when it must come . . .":

> "Why, take yourself, Sir Leicester Dedlock, Baronet. If there's a blow to be inflicted on you, you naturally think of your family. You ask yourself, how would all them

ancestors of yours, away to Julius Caesar—not to go beyond him at present—have borne that blow; you remember scores of them that would have borne it well; and you
bear it well on their accounts, and to maintain the family
credit. That's the way you argue, and that's the way you
act." (Ch. 54)

There is an amusing cheekiness in this that reflects Dickens's flippant attitude toward the aristocracy, but there is
also a note of sincerity in Bucket's awareness that the revelation will inflict pain; he feels compassion for the human
tragedy regardless of its social milieu.

For all his comic use of flattery to cajole his victims,
Bucket is deeply serious in his dedication to arriving at the
truth. When he is about to wrap up the murder case,
Dickens describes him as "thoughtful" but "composed,
sure, confident. From the expression of his face he might
be a famous whist-player for a large stake—say a hundred
guineas certain—with the game in his hand, but with a
high reputation involved in his playing his hand out to the
last card in a masterly way" (Ch. 54). The interruption
by the despicable old moneylender Smallweed arouses
Bucket's scorn. To Smallweed's complaint that he wants
"more painstaking and search-making into this murder,"
Bucket wags his famous forefinger and intentionally
adopts a tone of fierce anger:

"Now I tell you what," says Mr. Bucket . . . "I am damned
if I am a-going to have my case spoilt, or interfered with, or
anticipated by so much as half a second of time by
any human being in creation. *You* want more painstaking

and search-making! *You* do? Do you see this hand, and do you think that *I* don't know the right time to stretch it out and put it on the arm that fired that shot?"

Such is the dread power of the man, and so terribly evident it is that he makes no idle boast, that Mr. Small-weed begins to apologize. Mr. Bucket, dismissing his sudden anger, checks him.

"The advice I give you is, don't you trouble your head about the murder. That's my affair." (Ch. 54)

This is not a display of petulant egotism on Bucket's part; he takes pride in his work, calling it "a beautiful case," and he wants nothing to interfere with its proper solution.

After the arrest of Hortense for the murder of Tulkinghorn, Bucket engages in a cogent summary of the case that anticipates Sherlock Holmes and all his successors. First, Bucket declares that he was never convinced of the guilt of the soldier George but had to arrest him because the evidence against him was too strong to ignore. Next, he was forced to suspect Lady Dedlock because she was seen by George on the stairs at the time of the murder and because he knows the secret of her hatred of Tulkinghorn. Finally, he explains how he set a trap for Mademoiselle Hortense, who with Dickensian coincidence happened to be lodging with Bucket and his wife. With the aid of Mrs. Bucket, a "lady of natural detective genius," Hortense's attempts to incriminate Lady Dedlock are discovered. Mrs. Bucket sees Hortense both write and post the letters in which Hortense accused her former mistress of committing the murder. The wadding from the gun that killed Tulkinghorn was torn from a printed sheet belonging to

Hortense and retrieved by Mrs. Bucket to provide evidence of its source. Most important, the gun itself is retrieved from the pond near the place where Hortense and Mrs. Bucket had tea on the afternoon of Tulkinghorn's funeral, providing the final proof needed for Bucket to complete his case.

Having solved the murder mystery, however, Bucket finds that his work is not yet done. Lady Dedlock has fled and must be found, and Bucket takes over the search with supreme confidence: "Sir Leicester Dedlock, Baronet, what you've trusted to me I'll go through with. Don't you be afraid of my turning out of my way, right or left, or taking a sleep, or a wash, or a shave till I have found what I go in search of" (Ch. 56). He quickly examines Lady Dedlock's boudoir, finding Esther Summerson's handkerchief and going at once to ask Esther to accompany him in the search for her mother.

Esther describes their visit to the police station at half-past one in the morning, where Dickens's idealization of the London police appears. The police officers "in their perfectly neat uniforms" are "quietly writing at their desks" or acting upon Bucket's whispered instructions, impressing Esther with the calm efficiency of the whole operation. They next visit the Thames River Police, where Bucket ascertains that the latest body is not that of Lady Dedlock, and where Esther observes that "everybody seemed to know and defer to" Mr. Bucket.

During the long journey through the night that follows, Esther notes Bucket's methods in following the trail of the missing woman:

He had gone into every late or early public-house where there was a light . . . and had got down to talk to the turnpike-keepers. I had heard him ordering drink, and chinking money, and making himself agreeable and merry everywhere; but whenever he took his seat upon the box again, his face resumed its watchful steady look, and he always said to the driver in the same business tone, "Get on, my lad!" (Ch. 57)

Following the trail to St. Albans and to the brickmakers' cottage, Bucket exerts his detective powers to deduce that the surly husbands of Liz and Jenny have Lady Dedlock's watch, else why should they talk about "twenty minutes past" and "having no watch to tell the time by"? He deduces that the watch was a bribe, but he cannot be sure of its purpose. Hence he continues on a false trail for some time until he theorizes that Lady Dedlock and Jenny have exchanged clothes. Reversing direction, he turns back toward London, correctly guessing Lady Dedlock's destination; and indeed they find her lying dead at the gate of the cemetery where her lover was buried.

Historians of mystery fiction who accord to Sergeant Cuff in Collins's *The Moonstone* the title of father of English detectives may fail to note that Inspector Bucket appeared some seven or eight years before Cuff. Both characters derive from the same source—the London Detective Police—but is was Dickens, not Collins, who set the pattern. In the mutual influence of these two friends and collaborators, Collins took his cue from Dickens in the creation of the admirable detective, whereas it was Collins who inspired Dickens to take a keener interest in suspense plotting, an influence that became more evident from 1859 onward.

At the very time Dickens was formulating plans for a new novel which was to become *Great Expectations* (1861), Collins's *The Woman in White* was running as a serial in Dickens's own magazine *All the Year Round*. Constantly before Dickens's eyes was the frenzied enthusiasm of the readers and the gratifying increase in circulation which put more money than ever into Collins's pocket. It is impossible not to see a connection between this object lesson and the element of surprise that he introduced so successfully into his new novel. In *Great Expectations*, when Pip learns that his benefactor is not Miss Havisham but the convict Magwitch, the reader is as genuinely shocked as Pip himself. The opening scene with the terrified little Pip bringing food to the escaped convict has been forgotten, and the revelation that at first seems to destroy all Pip's hopes of rising in the social scale and winning the love of Estella becomes instead the turning point in his moral growth. The greatness of the novel does not of course depend upon the device of plot, but the sustaining of the surprise element does contribute to a tighter and more artistic construction in *Great Expectations* than in any of Dickens's earlier novels.

The same influence from Collins became even more explicit when the popularity of *The Moonstone* (1868) inspired Dickens to try his hand at the same form in *The Mystery of Edwin Drood*. There is little doubt that Dickens was slightly dismayed at the success of *The Moonstone*, which was running to wild acclaim in *All the Year Round*. Collins was, after all, the younger writer, and no master wishes to be oustripped in public favor by his protegé, especially when he himself is the greater artist. Whatever Dickens's thought processes, there was a clear declaration of competition in running a new novel with the word "mystery" in its title in the pages of the same magazine that had just published a best-selling mystery. Perhaps the most frustrating aspect of *Drood*'s unfinished state, for readers then and now, is that we shall never know how well Dickens might have succeeded in outdoing his friend in the creation of a mystery plot.

THE MYSTERY OF EDWIN DROOD

When Dickens died he had finished just half of the projected twelve monthly parts of *Edwin Drood*, and there were no notes to indicate how the plot would have been worked out had he lived to complete it. Ever since 1870 readers have engaged in a lively controversy over Dickens's intentions; a whole "Drood industry" has arisen and is still active today, sifting and analyzing the meager clues available to us.

Dickens returned to his childhood memories of the cathedral town of Rochester, called Cloisterham in the novel, for the setting of *Drood*. The tone is somber, haunting, almost elegiac, as the old cathedral and its precincts are lovingly described. Mysterious goings-on occur from the opening scene, in which John Jasper, the respectable cathedral choirmaster, is seen taking opium in a London den run by a cryptic old woman who listens to his drugged dreams with unseemly attention. An aura of the exotic East hovers over the story: a brother and sister, Helena and Neville Landless, come from Ceylon to stay with Canon Crisparkle. Jasper's nephew, Edwin Drood, is slated to go as an engineer to Egypt, where the Drood family has business interests. A stonemason named Durdles roams about the cathedral, mysteriously tapping walls in the crypt and adjacent tombs. Jasper makes nocturnal visits to the cathedral tower with Durdles, plying him with drink, noting the keys in his bundle, and showing interest in a pile of quicklime on the premises.

Matters are complicated by elements of romance. In a reverse of the Montague and Capulet tradition, the fathers of Edwin and Rosa Bud had imposed an engagement upon the young people, which both find irksome. Edwin is attracted to Helena; Rosa and a young man named Tartar become mutually attracted. The lawyer Grewgious (the first "good" member of that profession in Dickens's fiction) gives Edwin a ring to be given to Rosa but which Edwin retains in his pocket when Rosa breaks off their engagement.

Such are the ingredients of the mystery plot when Edwin Drood disappears. Although Jasper insists that his nephew was murdered and accuses Neville Landless of the crime, the reader is guided to suspect Jasper, whose motive is his hopeless passion for Rosa. A stranger named Dick Datchery arrives in Cloisterham and devotes himself to a surveillance of Jasper. At this point the fragment ends, leaving a tantalizing series of unanswered questions for posterity.

There have been many attempts at sequels or completions of *Edwin Drood*. One enterprising publisher brought out a volume entitled "John Jasper's Secret," falsely purporting it to be written by Wilkie Collins and Charles Dickens, Junior. The author of one sequel claimed that it was dictated by the spirit of Dickens himself. The attempt to reproduce Dickens's style renders most such work invalid. Even the recent completion by Leon Garfield, perhaps the best effort to date, tries to accomplish what is, in effect, the impossible.[13]

More significant are the many theories about the ending, based upon a variety of sources. The chief controversy concerns the question of whether Edwin Drood was, in fact, murdered or whether he is alive and will reappear in the novel. A secondary controversy concerns the identity of Dick Datchery—is he another character in disguise or is he a character in his own right? Looking at these issues in turn will give an indication of the nature of the Drood material and suggest some of the pros and cons of the arguments.

Whether or not they are mystery fans, readers share an almost universal reaction that might be expressed in the question, "So what is the mystery?" It seems so obvious that John Jasper is set up as the murderer of his nephew Edwin that readers promptly divide into two groups, those who shrug and say that Dickens apparently did not care much about the mystery plot anyway, and those who say that of course there must be a surprise in store or he would not have used the word "mystery" in the title. If

Dickens was going to outdo Wilkie Collins, they argue, he would surely have created a plot with a series of ingenious twists like that of *The Moonstone*. Conflicting evidence appears on both sides of the question from three major sources: the testimony of Dickens's friends and family, the testimony of his notes for the novel, and the testimony of the text of the novel itself.

The first piece of external evidence about Dickens's intentions comes from John Forster's *Life of Charles Dickens*, the three volumes of which were published from 1872 to 1874. Dickens wrote to Forster in August 1869 that he had "a very curious and new idea for [his] new story. Not a communicable one (or the interest of the book would be gone), but a very strong one, though difficult to work."[14] Forster then continues with a passage which has formed the basis for much of the battle over *Drood:*

> The story, I learnt immediately afterward, was to be that of the murder of a nephew by his uncle; the originality of which was to consist in the review of the murderer's career by himself at the close, when its temptations were to be dwelt upon as if, not he the culprit, but some other man, were the tempted. The last chapters were to be written in the condemned cell, to which his wickedness, all elaborately elicited from him as if told of another, had brought him. Discovery by the murderer of the utter needlessness of the murder for its object, was to follow hard upon commission of the deed; but all discovery of the murderer was to be baffled till towards the close, when, by means of a gold ring which had resisted the corrosive effects of the lime into which he had thrown the body, not only the

person murdered was to be identified but the locality of
the crime and the man who committed it.[15]

At first glance this would appear to settle the whole question, if we accept at face value Forster's account of Dickens's plot for the novel.

But is Forster to be relied upon in this instance? Dickens's letter to Forster clearly states that he does not intend
to reveal the "new idea" for his story, for "the interest of
the book would be gone." Yet Forster would have us believe that "immediately afterward" Dickens proceeded to
tell him the whole plot. In the past Dickens had frequently talked over his stories with his friend, but his letter seems to tell Forster that this time he does *not* wish to
reveal his story in advance. Why would Forster claim that
Dickens had told him all? For the simple human reason
that his great weakness in his otherwise genuine friendship
with Dickens was his desire to occupy a position of special
privilege; he must prove to the world that among all of
Dickens's friends he was the only one entrusted with con-
fidences which were withheld from the others.[16]

The evidence of Dickens's daughter Kate supports Forster's statement about *Edwin Drood* largely on the ground
that her father would not have lied to his old friend. In a
magazine article in 1906, some thirty-five years after
her father's death, Kate replied to critics who had suggested that Dickens might have withheld knowledge of his
plot from everyone, including Forster. Acknowledging
that Forster, while "devotedly attached" to her father,
was "a little jealous of his confidence and more than a little

exacting in his demands upon it,[17] she points out that Forster would have been thoroughly incensed if Dickens had deceived him and that her father would not have wished to distress his old friend in that way.

In reply to the suggestion that Edwin Drood was not dead, Kate comes out firmly in support of his having been murdered by Jasper. First, she agrees with Forster that her father did not intend to rely upon "the Mystery alone . . . for the interest and originality of his idea" but rather upon "the psychological description the murderer gives us of his temptations, temperament, and character, as if told by another." Next, she states that her brother Charles "had heard from his father's lips that Edwin Drood was dead." Finally, she quotes her Aunt Georgina as having asked, "I hope you haven't really killed poor Edwin Drood?" to which Dickens replied, "I call my book the Mystery, not the History, of Edwin Drood."[18]

Forster's and Kate's evidence has been countered in a number of ways. Dickens may have intended to reveal the full truth to Forster later on in the writing of the novel but well before the conclusion, thus allowing him to be "in the know" before anyone else. As for Charles and Aunt Georgina, the very fact that they, like many readers of *Drood*, wondered about Edwin's fate suggests in itself that his murder is in doubt. If Drood was indeed murdered by Jasper, as the text of the novel hints, then what is the secret that Dickens so jealously guarded, even from his family? Charles Dickens, Junior later declared that when he asked if Edwin Drood was murdered, his father looked astonished and said, "What else do you suppose?"[19] Dickens's response to Charles by meeting his question with a question may be interpreted, not as confirmation, but as avoiding commitment. Similarly, Dickens's reply to Aunt Georgina may be seen as cryptic. If Drood's story is a "Mystery, not a History," it is also clearly not "The *Murder* of Edwin Drood." So far from confirming Edwin's murder, Dickens's replies leave the question wide open.

The evidence of the illustrations for *Edwin Drood* further compounds the mystery. Kate's husband Charles Allston Collins designed the wrapper of the monthly parts according to instructions given by Dickens but with no information about the plot. The cover design, consisting of a series of sketches surrounding the central title, has created endless disagreement among Droodists, each theorist identifying the figures to suit his particular reading of the novel (see Frontispiece). The woman and the Chinaman in the lower corners of the picture are surely the persons in the opium dens, but who are the couple walking away from the church, or the man wooing the girl in the garden, or the girl gazing at the poster reading "Lost," or the three figures climbing the circular staircase? Most puzzling is the lower central scene in which a man carrying a lantern seems startled to encounter another man in the place he has just entered. If the man with the lantern is Jasper, is it Edwin whom he encounters, or Edwin's ghost, or Datchery, or someone disguised as Datchery? Is their meeting place the tomb where Jasper has left (or believes he has left) Edwin's body? The conjectures are endless, and the fact that Charles Collins himself did not know the answers confirms that Dickens was bent upon keeping to himself the secret of his plot.

When Charles Collins's health did not allow him to continue with the illustrations, Dickens obtained the services of the artist Luke Fildes. Two pieces of evidence offered by Fildes appear to confirm that Jasper murdered Edwin. An interview with Fildes published in the *Strand Magazine* in 1893 quoted him as saying that Dickens had asked him to visit a Rochester jail so that he could draw Jasper in the condemned cell.[20] In 1905 Fildes stated that Dickens had required Jasper to be shown wearing a long black neckerchief, for "Jasper strangles Edwin Drood with it."[21] The best counter to such evidence is the theory that Jasper attempted to strangle Edwin with the black scarf, believed that he had succeeded, and was unaware that Edwin had somehow escaped.

Although Dickens left no information about how the plot was to continue, he did leave some working notes on the novel up to the point where the story breaks off. Also among his papers was a list of tentative titles for the novel, dated "Friday, Twentieth August, 1869," shortly before he began writing the first number. The list contains seventeen projected titles:

The loss of James Edwyn Wakefield

James's Disappearance

Flight and Pursuit

Sworn to avenge it

One Object in Life

A Kinsman's Devotion

The Two Kinsmen

The Loss of Edwyn Brood
The loss of Edwin Brude
The Mystery in the Drood Family
The loss of Edwyn Drood
The flight of Edwyn Drood
Edwin Drood in hiding
The Loss of Edwin Drude
The Disappearance of Edwin Drood
The Mystery of Edwin Drood
Dead? or alive?

Many of the titles bear on the question of whether Edwin Drood was murdered or is still alive, but far from resolving the issue, they may be interpreted as support for either side. Words like "loss" and "disappearance" may be said to sustain the view that the surprise element will be the revelation that Edwin was indeed murdered. On the other hand, phrases like "Edwin Drood in hiding" or in "flight" are impossible to reconcile with any theory except that of his being alive and destined to return.

Other titles in the list strongly suggest that a large part of the undisclosed plot will concern a mystery in the Drood family, no doubt involving the forebears of both Jasper and Edwin. The "Devotion" of one of the "Two Kinsmen" seems to echo Jasper's either true or feigned devotion to Edwin. Someone must be "Sworn to avenge" some crime arising out of a family feud. The "One Object in Life" in the novel as we have it is Jasper's avowed dedication to finding Edwin's murderer, an ironic statement if he is indeed himself the guilty man.

In addition to the projected titles for the novel, Dickens's notes for the ensuing chapters present equally baffling clues. Two of these appear to confirm that murder is planned. Under Chapter II we find "Uncle and Nephew" and "Murder very far off" and under "Chapter XI, A Night with 'Durdles,'" "Lay the ground for the manner of the Murder, to come out at last."

On the other hand, the title of Chapter XIV, "When Shall These Three Meet Again?" is followed by the names of Neville, Edwin, and Jasper, as each "goes up the Postern stair" to their Christmas Eve meeting. The echo from *Macbeth* may suggest the theme of murder, but conversely the chapter title gives the reader an ineradicable impression that these three *are* destined to come together again.

In the light of the external evidence from Dickens's friends and family and from his own notes to the novel, no one could be faulted for following the traditional view that Forster's summary of the plot of *Edwin Drood* was correct. This would mean that the great secret Dickens was so anxious to preserve was not Jasper's guilt (which would be assumed) but the discovery of the ring on Edwin's body, the only object not consumed by the quicklime. This would also mean that Kate was right when she confirmed that the chief interest of the story was not to be the mystery itself but the psychological study of the criminal in the condemned cell. Together with the evidence of Luke Fildes and others, cited above, this view has much to recommend it and may indeed be a valid solution.

On the other hand, the opposing view holds that if Dickens wanted to compete with Wilkie Collins, he was going to have to do better than that and somehow keep

Edwin alive. The first major argument for Edwin's survival was set forth in 1887 by the astronomer Richard A. Proctor, who suggested that Dickens planned to use again in *Drood* his theme of someone being "watched by the dead."[22] Among many examples of this theme in Dickens's work, Proctor cites the play, *No Thoroughfare*, written in collaboration with Wilkie Collins, in which the villain Obenreizer believes that he has killed Vendale, only to be confronted by the missing man in a dramatic climax highly suggestive of Jasper's confrontation of a living Edwin in *Drood*. Similarly, in *Our Mutual Friend* (1865) John Harmon is believed to be dead but reappears. In Proctor's theory, Jasper believes that he has strangled Edwin, but Edwin escapes and returns, disguised as Datchery, to spy upon his uncle. While Edwin-as-Datchery is not altogether convincing, Proctor's initial conjecture that Jasper does attempt to murder Edwin is shared by many subsequent theorists who believe Edwin to be still alive. The obvious merit of the survival theory is that it accommodates both Jasper's presumed guilt and the compelling evidence that Dickens did have a surprise ending in store.

Other evidence that Edwin is still alive derives from the text of the novel itself. For example, Clement Shorter in 1911 commented that "Dickens would never have allowed us to be interested in the personality of Edwin as we are in the early chapters had he not intended him to return in the end and give the whole story a pleasant, romantic wind-up."[23] Developing Shorter's brief comment in more detail, we note that if Dickens planned to have Edwin murdered, it would seem pointless for him not only to make Edwin appealing but to carefully create the impression that Edwin is falling in love with Helena Landless. Yet he does so by alluding not once but three times to Edwin's growing interest in Helena. After their first meeting we are told that Edwin is already "impressed by Helena"; later he tells Grewgious that "she is a strikingly handsome girl"; and finally, after the delicate little scene in which Rosa and Edwin agree not to marry, we are told that "he did already entertain some wandering speculations whether it might ever come to pass that he would know more of Miss Landless." For an incurable romantic like Dickens, this fairly cries out "Foreshadowing!" Moreover, it occurs near the end of Chapter 13, immediately before Edwin's disappearance. Since Dickens was too skillful an artist to include such material carelessly, it is difficult to believe that he intended to kill off Edwin in the next chapter.

Even more significant than the promised romance with Helena Landless is the implied theme that Edwin is the flawed hero who must learn humility before he comes to full maturity. Many Dickens critics have noted that a sign of his developing artistry is the increasing quality of change in his central characters, yet no one seems to have observed its application to the character of Edwin Drood. An early hero like Oliver Twist was quite simply a "good child" victimized by society, who does not change in the course of the novel. David Copperfield shows more evidence of growth, beginning as a childhood innocent and learning through experience to adopt more mature values. In the last two novels before *Drood* the theme of moral growth becomes dominant. In *Great Expectations* Pip's thoughtless arrogance must give way to a recognition of the moral values represented by Joe Gargery, before Pip achieves maturity. In *Our Mutual Friend* the theme is transferred to the heroine, Bella Wilfer, who must learn to reject her craving for money and material possessions before she is worthy of her suitor, John Harmon.

Everything we see about Edwin Drood suggests that he too will pass through some initiatory rites before achieving manhood. At first Edwin is likable but unthinkingly self-centered. He describes himself early in the novel with disarming frankness to Jasper: "I am afraid I am but a shallow, surface kind of fellow, Jack, and that my headpiece is none of the best. But I needn't say I am young; and perhaps I shall not grow worse as I grow older" (Ch. 2). Canon Crisparkle, whose word is reliable, confirms Edwin's essential goodness; he tells Neville Landless that despite his shortcomings Edwin's is "a frank, good-natured character" and that he "can trust to it for that" (Ch. 10). Unlike Neville, whose childhood has been harsh, Edwin has never known adversity. When the two young men quarrel over Edwin's cavalier attitude toward Rosa, Neville exclaims that "It might have been better for Mr. Drood to have known some hardships," creating the strong impression that Dickens intends for Edwin to endure some bitter experiences in future that will test his strength. That Edwin has potential for growth is carefully laid out in the scene in which Grewgious gently reproves him for his flippant treatment of Rosa. Edwin feels the sting of the criticism but also its justice:

He had a conscience, and Mr. Grewgious had pricked it. That gentleman's steady convictions of what was right and what was wrong in such a case as his were neither to be frowned aside nor laughed aside. . . . Once put into this narrowed way of action, it was curious that he began to consider Rosa's claims upon him more unselfishly than he had ever considered them before and began to be less sure of himself than he had ever been in all his easy-going days. (Ch. 13)

Echoes of Pip are unmistakable here. Like Pip, Edwin is charming but heedless of the feelings of others; bit by bit, we see the beginnings of awareness and self-questioning; ultimately, we assume, he will achieve the maturity that will make him a worthy mate for the resourceful Helena. Since Dickens built up such promise for Edwin's future, we are the more inclined to believe that he intended for Edwin to have a future, at the same time creating a much more effective mystery plot.

This brings us to the question of Dick Datchery, who first appears in Chapter 18 of *The Mystery of Edwin Drood*. Six months have passed since Edwin's disappearance. The case against Neville Landless, spurred on by Jasper, has been dropped for lack of evidence. Meanwhile, Grewgious has been shown to suspect Jasper of some guilt in connection with Edwin. Chapter 18 begins:

At about this time a stranger appeared in Cloisterham, a white-haired personage, with black eyebrows. Being buttoned up in a tightish surtout, with a buff waistcoat and grey trousers, he had something of a military air; but he announced himself at the hotel . . . as an idle dog who lived upon his means; and he farther announced that he had a mind to take a lodging in the picturesque old city for a month or two.

Datchery's white head "was unusually large, and his shock of white hair was unusually thick and ample," and on one occasion he claps his hand on his head, believing that he is wearing the hat which is actually in his hand. Hence, many Drood theorists believe that he is wearing a wig and is therefore in disguise. Accordingly, he has been identified variously as Edwin, Helena, Neville, Grewgious, Bazzard, Tartar, Grewgious's fellow solicitor—in short, as almost everyone who has already appeared in the novel. That Datchery, whoever he (or she) is, comes to Cloisterham to spy upon Jasper is certain. He takes a room with the Topeses from which he can view Jasper's comings and goings, making "uncouth chalked strokes" on the cupboard door to indicate the degree of his success in surveillance. Musing to himself, he remarks that he likes "the old tavern way of keeping scores. Illegible except to the scorer" (Ch. 23).

A glance at a few of the Datchery theories will suggest the ingenuity as well as the variety of the guesses about who Datchery might be.

Richard A. Proctor's theory, noted above, was that Datchery is Edwin himself, coming back to collect evidence of his uncle's treachery. The principal objection to Edwin as Datchery is that he has little motive for disguising himself and seeking information about Jasper. If he knows that Jasper attempted to murder him, he has only to expose him, at the same time clearing Neville Landless of suspicion, especially for the sake of Helena, whom Edwin wishes to marry.

The case for Helena Landless as Datchery was first presented by J. Cuming Walters in 1905.[24] Based largely upon Neville's information that Helena had disguised herself as a boy on more than one occasion when she and her twin brother were children, and supplemented by the strong motive that Helena possesses for clearing her beloved brother from suspicion, the Helena theory is an ingenious one. It was hailed as "brilliant" by Sir W. Robertson Nicoll, whose 1912 study of *Edwin Drood* not only supported Cuming Walters's Helena theory but added the detail that Datchery often appeared to keep his hands concealed, suggesting that Helena's hands would reveal her sex.[25] Unhappily for the Helena theory, Dickens's novel operates in a world of everyday reality, where no matter how willingly the reader suspends his disbelief, he cannot accept the possibility that a young girl who is "lithe" and "very dark and rich in colour, of almost the gipsy type" could convincingly appear as a bluff retired military man who scores up crude chalk strokes in the "old tavern" manner when no one is watching him. At a distance, with or without hands, she might have pulled off such a deception, but in conversation with Jasper and others who knew her in Cloisterham, she would have been recognized at once by her voice if not by her appearance.

Among other candidates for the post of Datchery-in-disguise, Grewgious is nominated by Richard M. Baker in his 1948 study of *Drood.*[26] Despite Baker's persuasive arguments, it is difficult to imagine the angular and diffident solicitor turning up as the affable and easy-mannered Datchery. As for Grewgious' clerk, Bazzard, the candidate of Felix Aylmer (1965) and others, this thin, misanthropic young man is not only physically unsuited to the role but would need no disguise in Cloisterham, for he is not known to anyone there.

The most obvious problem in identifying either Helena or Grewgious as Datchery is that both are living in London and visible to others there. Their proponents are forced to ignore the fact that Datchery moves into the room at the Topeses' and is seen there daily, while at the same time Grewgious is in his London chambers and Helena has just come to London to stay with her brother. Only Edwin, if he has returned to "watch from the dead," or Bazzard, who is mysteriously absent at this time, could physically occupy Datchery's lodging, and neither is a convincing candidate.

Who, then, is Dick Datchery? The obvious answer is that Datchery is a detective who had been hired by someone (probably Grewgious) to obtain evidence against Jasper. Despite the ingenuity of the other theories, the best solution still seems to be that he is in fact a detective and not another character in disguise. His shock of thick white hair, which he conspicuously shakes like a Newfoundland dog on every occasion, is not necessarily a wig but more likely a descriptive Dickensian tag, for one would suppose that a person wearing an unfamiliar wig would avoid shaking his head lest he dislodge the wig.

Furthermore, Datchery appears to be genuinely a stranger in Cloisterham. He asks directions to the Topeses' lodgings but soon "became bewildered, and went boggling about and about the Cathedral tower" until Deputy comes to his rescue. Since his confusion is reported only by the omniscient narrator and is not assumed for the benefit of an observer, he cannot be Edwin, Helena, or Grewgious, all of whom are familiar with the town. Only Bazzard might lose his way, and he has no need for a disguise in Cloisterham.

Once Datchery is accepted as a character in his own right, he fits naturally into the plan of the novel. Not only Dickens himself but most of his readers were fresh from a reading of Collins's *The Moonstone*, in which Sergeant Cuff displayed his techniques and his eccentricities. Given Dickens's interest in the London Detective Police, his own creation of the inimitable Inspector Bucket, and his awareness of the popularity of Sergeant Cuff, what is more likely than that he should put a detective into his own mystery story? Datchery is just the sort of bluff and genial chap that one would expect to find in this role. Already endowed with suitable eccentricities, he will surely play a major role in solving the mystery. With Dickensian coincidence he may well turn out to have some connection with the mystery in the Drood family, thus having a personal as well as a professional motive for his detective services. In any case, his being a genuine detective is more convincing and places less strain on the reader's credulity than any of the efforts to present him as someone in disguise.

While it is impossible to describe even a fraction of the many attempts that have been made to solve the *Mystery of Edwin Drood*, a few representative solutions will illustrate the ingenuity of the solvers.

The actor Felix Aylmer, in his study of *Drood* cited above, offers the unique argument that Jasper is not evil at all but will turn out to be maligned and misunderstood. His devotion to Edwin, which we assume to be feigned, is real, and he will eventually win the love of Rosa Bud. Improbable as his theory appears, Aylmer offers a closely supported argument, including some interesting conjectures about the Drood family feud and its origins in Moslem customs.

A clever but little known essay by Harry B. Smith entitled "Sherlock Holmes Solves the Mystery of Edwin Drood" first appeared in 1924 and has recently been reprinted.[27] When presented with the Drood case, the Great Detective concludes that Jasper attempts to strangle Edwin with the black scarf but falls into an opium-induced seizure. Edwin, believing his uncle to be insane, rushes off to Egypt, stopping first to tell Grewgious what has occurred. Jasper awakens and believes that he has murdered Edwin and put his body in the tomb, just as he had dreamed hundreds of times. The cover illustration, therefore, portrays Jasper confronting Edwin in the tomb, for Holmes says that obviously the only solution with sufficient drama is that of "the would-be murderer and his supposed victim face to face."[28]

The solution of the noted mystery writer John Dickson Carr, from a previously unpublished letter, is recorded in a recent issue of *The Armchair Detective*.[29] Carr's ingenious theory was that Edwin was murdered but not by Jasper; the culprit is Helena Landless, who is dressed in her twin brother's clothing and carries a heavy walking stick like his. Mistaking her for Neville, Edwin engages in a struggle with her, and she strikes him fatally with the weapon in her hand. Jasper, who has suffered an opium blackout, recovers in time to see Edwin's body and believes he has killed him.

Another theory, unpublished to date, is that after Neville Landless leaves Edwin on the night of the supposed murder, Edwin is approached by a young stranger (perhaps a cousin who resembles Edwin) and is told of some crisis in the family that requires his immediate presence in Egypt. Edwin asks the cousin to tell his uncle Jasper where he has gone, giving him the ring to be returned to Grewgious. When Edwin has gone, Jasper comes upon the cousin in the dark and strangles him, mistaking him for Edwin, and puts his body in the tomb. This theory has the merit of making Jasper in fact guilty of murder, while allowing Edwin to return, and also accounting for the finding of the ring on the body which Jasper had covered with quicklime.[30]

In addition to the major questions concerning Edwin and Datchery, the novel leaves many other puzzles unsolved, such as the identity of the old opium woman who takes an ominous interest in Jasper, or the answer to what Jasper sees at the foot of the Cathedral tower in his dream, and so on. From his earliest fiction Dickens delighted in gathering up seemingly disparate threads of plot and revealing them as coincidentally related. Whatever the surprise in store in *Drood*, we may be certain that the plot was carefully planned. Of all the nineteenth-century writers who contributed in one way or another to the development of mystery fiction, Dickens was by far the greatest literary genius. It is regrettable that this last great work, with its brilliant characters and haunting setting remains an unsolved mystery.

4

Joseph Sheridan Le Fanu: Horror and Suspense

While some Victorian writers might be said to write mystery fiction laced with elements of Gothic terror, Sheridan Le Fanu's fiction can be more aptly described as tales of terror with elements of mystery and suspense. He is equally known for his ghost stories and for his realistic fiction, and in both his roots go back to the Gothic tradition in English fiction and to its chief American expression in the horror tales of Poe. In his two finest novels, *Wylder's Hand* and *Uncle Silas*, both published in 1864, he brings the tale of horror and suspense to a height not matched by any other novelist in English.

Born in Dublin in 1814, Le Fanu was descended on his father's side from a Huguenot family that had settled in Ireland in the seventeeth century, and on his mother's side from the Sheridans of literary fame, including the dramatist Richard Brinsley Sheridan.[1] Le Fanu's father was a clergyman in the Church of England, holding the position of resident chaplain of the Royal Hibernian School in Phoenix Park in Dublin at the time Joseph was born. The three children—a daughter Catherine, Joseph, and a younger brother, William—spent their early years in the picturesque parkland, watching the soldiers of the Royal Irish Artillery drilling and hearing of occasional duels near the banks of the Liffey, a setting later commemorated by Joseph in *The House by the Churchyard*.

In 1826 the family moved to Abington in County Limerick, where the father was rector and dean of Emly. The boys were spared the rigors of a public school, reading lessons with their father and with a lenient tutor who often preferred fishing to study, while Joseph's own studious inclinations led him to read widely on his own. The freedom to roam the wild hills and glens of the neighborhood and to absorb the folk tales of the country people gave Joseph a rich source for his later fiction.

In 1831, with the beginning of the tithe wars, the idyllic childhood days were shaken by political conflict. An uprising against paying tithes to the Anglo-Irish Church made the dean and his family the targets of personal attack. On one occasion the boys escaped a stoning which might have been fatal. Like many another Anglo-Irish family, the Le Fanus, as members of the ascendancy class, felt at times a sentimental sympathy with the Irish rebels but were unshaken in their belief that British rule was best for the Irish people, a paternalism that may have been misguided but was none the less sincere.

In due course, Joseph attended Trinity College, University of Dublin, engaging in debates and moving in a circle of young intellectuals. Despite his conservative background, he wrote a sentimental patriotic ballad entitled "Shamus O'Brien," in which the rebel hero escapes the gallows, a poem which enjoyed considerable popularity when it was published in 1850. Meanwhile, after receiving his degree with Honors in Classics, Le Fanu read law and was called to the Irish bar in 1839, but like Wilkie Collins in England, he never practiced that profession. Le Fanu turned instead to journalism and became the editor and owner of various Dublin newspapers and magazines over the next twenty-five years. His first short story, "The Ghost and the Bone-Setter," was published in 1838 in the *Dublin University Magazine*, a journal Le Fanu later owned and to which he continued to contribute short stories and novels until he sold it in 1869.

In 1843, Le Fanu married Susanna Bennet,[2] the attractive daughter of a Dublin barrister. The couple enjoyed an active social life and were devoted to their family of two daughters and two sons. In 1850 they lived for a time with Susanna's parents in their fine old house in Merrion Square, then a fashionable area of Dublin, and retained the lease of the house when the Bennets left Ireland to settle in Shropshire. Susanna's sudden death in 1858, at the age of thirty-five, left Le Fanu shocked and grief-stricken. He wrote to his mother: "The greatest misfortune of my life has overtaken me. My darling wife is gone. . . . She was the light of my life. . . . I adored her."[3]

In the 1840s Le Fanu published two novels, *The Cock and the Anchor* (1845) and *The Fortunes of Colonel Torlough*

O'Brien (1847), both Irish historical romances in the manner of Sir Walter Scott, laced with scenes of violence suggestive of the school of Harrison Ainsworth. For the next decade, he published short stories and journalistic pieces but did not return to the novel form until the 1860s, when he was inspired by Wilkie Collins's *The Woman in White* to try a new approach in fiction. After his wife's death, Le Fanu had gradually withdrawn from society and become something of a recluse, seeing only family members and a few intimate friends. Known in his final years as "the invisible Prince," he devoted himself to his fiction, often writing late at night and into the small hours of the morning.

The first three works of the 1860s—*The House by the Churchyard*, *Wylder's Hand*, and *Uncle Silas*—comprise his best achievements in the novel form. Although he produced some excellent short stories during his later years, the quality of his novels declined after 1865, perhaps because of his growing reluctance to fill the requisite three volumes that publishers demanded for the novel. The stranglehold of the circulating libraries, with their insistence upon the three-decker, was not broken until nearly the end of the century. Le Fanu worked best at this time in the medium of the short story or the intermediate-length novella. Since the big money was still in the novel market, many Victorian authors found it expedient to pad out their narratives until the increased pay for short stories from the 1890s onwards helped to change the pattern. Whatever the reasons, all of Le Fanu's later novels suffer from a sense of inflated length; the many fine characters and occasional scenes of great power are diminished by intervening passages of tedium and repetition. The solid craftsmanship that made *Wylder's Hand* and *Uncle Silas* so superb is only intermittently present in the later fiction.

In his last years, Le Fanu withdrew into a private world of study much like that of his character Austin Ruthyn in *Uncle Silas*, fascinated by Swedenborgian theories and reading widely in areas of the occult, vampire lore, and the like. A handsome and courtly gentleman to the end, he was remembered after his death in 1873 as "the beau ideal of an Irish wit and scholar of the old school."[4]

By definition, mystery fiction as a form excludes ghosts and the supernatural. From its inception in Edgar Allan Poe's supremely rational detective, Auguste Dupin, to Sherlock Holmes and his successors in the twentieth century, the genre requires that the solutions of crime puzzles be achieved without the intervention of occult forces. Thus we are not primarily concerned in this study with Le Fanu's supernatural fiction. A brief glance at the ghost stories that appeared off and on throughout his writing career will indicate their relationship to his other work.

For the aficionado of the ghostly, Le Fanu offers some fine reading. In the preface to a reissue of the collection titled *Madam Crowl's Ghost*, M. R. James pays him tribute: "He stands absolutely in the first rank as a writer of ghost stories. That is my deliberate verdict after reading all the supernatural tales I have been able to get hold of. Nobody sets the scene better than he, nobody touches in the effective detail more deftly."[5] Many of Le Fanu's stories derive from Irish folklore—children stolen by the fairies, visions, ghosts seeking revenge, sometimes Faustian tales of possession by the devil. Another group are what might be called realistic ghost stories, ones in which the settings and the events are related in such a matter-of-fact manner that the supernatural occurrences are all the more spine tingling. A fascinating feature of some stories is that, unlike Hamlet's mother, who was horrified to see her son gazing on the "uncorporeal air," the associates of the haunted persons may also see the ghosts. In "The Familiar" and in "Mr. Justice Harbottle," to cite two well-known stories, the apparitions are seen by servants and other characters as well as by the haunted persons. Some of the ghosts in these stories are metamorphic, changing into monkeys, dogs, owls, and so forth. Sometimes an old crime is revealed, as in "Madam Crowl's Ghost," in which the young servant girl sees the ghost of her mistress unlock a closet with its grisly contents. Perhaps the finest of these stories is "Carmilla," Le Fanu's venture into vampire lore, which inspired Bram Stoker's *Dracula* (1895). With its striking and unconventional lesbian theme of the beautiful young girl vampire preying upon young women, "Carmilla" is a brilliant and unique accomplishment.

All of the supernatural elements in Le Fanu's fiction appear in his short stories, not in the novels. The only exception occurs in *The Wyvern Mystery*, in which a mysterious black veil falling in front of the heroine is never explained, perhaps as the result of an oversight. Essentially, the novels are all written in a realistic mode, but Le Fanu's impulse toward the supernatural appears often in his creation of a ghostly atmosphere in novels where there are no ghosts. He is adept at creating eerie and macabre effects and often presents ghostlike apparitions that are rationally accounted for in the end.

One of Le Fanu's realistic short stories, without supernatural elements, is "The Evil Guest" (1851), a longer version of an earlier story entitled "Some Account of the Latter Days of the Hon. Richard Marston of Dunoran." Le Fanu had a curious habit of recycling stories, sometimes not once but twice. "The Evil Guest" became in its turn the three-volume novel *A Lost Name* (1868), and in this case the intermediate version is the best. A grisly but fascinating murder mystery, "The Evil Guest," comes complete with suspicion falling on an innocent person, a mystery concerning two murder weapons (why both a knife and a dagger?), an inquest, and some excellent characters, including a beautiful governess who is a femme fatale.

"The Evil Guest" illustrates the transitional nature of mystery fiction at mid-century. Because the story contains elements associated today with the mystery story, we can identify it as an early example of the form. However, the reader senses that Le Fanu's chief purpose in the story was the exposure of the evil wrought by the squire and that the murder is an example of his moral degradation rather than a puzzle set forth for the reader to solve. When the mystery story became a consciously contrived challenge with the central focus upon finding the solution to the problem posed—the form first popularized by Wilkie Collins in *The Woman in White*—the formula was established for modern mystery fiction.

In the first of Le Fanu's novels of the 1860s, *The House by the Churchyard* (1863), he seems to be experimenting with a number of modes, one of which is to follow Collins's lead and make an unsolved crime the focus of his story. The novel begins with the finding of a battered skull in a new grave in the churchyard. The narrator, Charles de Cresseron—an ancestral name that Le Fanu borrowed as a nom de plume under which the novel first appeared—recalls the incident from his childhood and now proposes to reconstruct the story of the murder with the aid of diaries and letters in his possession. The plot involves both the identification of the villain and his desperate attempts to cover up his crime of the distant past, even if he must kill again to do so, a plot that the reader is apt to find more transparent than the author might have wished. However, Le Fanu compensates for this by the skill with which he creates effective scenes of the macabre: the clandestine funeral in the church at midnight, the meeting of the suspect and the witnesses on the heath, the hand at the window pane echoing the ghost story at the Tiled House, and the unforgettable horror of the surgeon trepanning the skull of an apparently dying man.

The impulse toward writing a murder mystery, however, constitutes only one element in *The House by the Churchyard*. Le Fanu devotes much of the novel to recreating the social scene of the 1760s, a century earlier, in the then village of Chapelizod near Dublin, since immortalized in the fiction of James Joyce. Nostalgic memories of his childhood days in those delightful surroundings inspired Le Fanu to set his story among the people of the village and the officers of the Royal Irish Artillery. A good deal of comedy occurs in these scenes; some characters, like Magnolia McNamara and Lieutenant Fireworker O'Flaherty, are straight out of Dickens; others, like the general's sister Aunt Becky and her comic suitors, are reminiscent of Thackeray's social satire. As a counterpart to the comedy, there are occasional passages of tragic pathos, especially in the death of young Lilias Walsingham. The grief of her father, the rector, may indeed reflect Le Fanu's mourning for his wife. A surprising feature of the social fabric as it is presented in the novel is the absence of religious conflict. The Anglican clergyman, Reverend Walsingham, and the Catholic priest, Father Roach, appear to be on casually friendly terms with each other and with the townspeople, whose religious affiliations are never noted. Whether or not this was historically accurate, it does reflect Le Fanu's own implied view that political disturbances in Ireland did not materially affect people in their everyday relationships. Religious conflict never appears as a major issue in his fiction.

In addition to the elements of the mystery novel and the social novel, Le Fanu invests *The House by the Churchyard* with those ghostly trappings that become a characteristic of his realistic fiction, giving the impression that the novel contains supernatural elements that are not in fact there. Early in the novel, the description of the "Tiled House" begins in the best Gothic tradition: "It stood by a lonely bend of the narrow road. Lilias had often looked upon the short, straight, grass-grown avenue with an awful curiosity at the old house which she had learned in childhood to fear as the abode of shadowy tenants and unearthly dangers" (Ch. 11). When the old servant Sally speaks of the house being haunted, Lilias replies, "with a cosy little shudder," that while she does not believe in ghosts, she would be afraid to sleep in the house herself, for "the aerial image of the old house for a moment stood before her, with its peculiar malign, sacred, and skulking aspect, as if it had drawn back in shame and guilt under the melancholy old elms among the tall hemlock and nettles" (Ch. 11).

Hints of the supernatural are not satirized, they are simply expressed as something that sensible people find pleasantly titillating, but that are not to be taken literally. So it is with the splendid little ghost story which the narrator relates concerning the Tiled House. The last occupants of the house had fled from its precincts after being terrified by the menacing appearances of a plump white hand which rapped on doors, was seen at windows with its palm against the glass, and finally appeared to various members of the household as they lay in bed. Having told a most effective story, the narrator then apologizes to the reader for "loitering so long" over this sort of lore, thus removing it from the realm of "fact" but leaving a tantalizing aura of the ghostly (Ch. 12).

For all its rich variety, *The House by the Churchyard* suffers from a certain lack of coherence. Characters and events are sometimes introduced but not fully developed. There is no central character, either hero or heroine, with whom the reader can form a bond. A mysterious young Mr. Mervyn, who becomes the tenant of the Tiled

House, is ambiguous enough to play the role of hero but is almost forgotten throughout the course of the novel until he emerges in the final segment as the suitor of Gertrude Chattesworth, the local beauty. Young Captain Devereux comes closer to the status of hero, albeit a faulty one; the expectation that he may gain some sort of redemption through his love for Lilias Walsingham is negated by her death, which seems more fortuitous than intrinsic to the moral fabric of the novel. The title itself is disconcerting, for its promise of concentration upon a particular house is not fulfilled; indeed, Le Fanu refers in passing to the home of Sturk, the artillery surgeon, as "The House by the Churchyard," although this house has no distinguishing features of particular interest in the story.

The inconsistency in tone in *The House by the Churchyard* suggests that Le Fanu was not sure whether he wanted to write a comic novel or a novel of suspense and was in fact exploring both modes. Nevertheless, the novelist Elizabeth Bowen, in her introduction to *House*, notes that despite what she calls these "oscillations between sinister grimness and full-blooded jocosity," the novel displays those qualities of excellence which mark Le Fanu's fiction, his "curious, near-visionary manner of seeing and way of writing, his what one might call depth-charge perceptions into feeling and motive . . . with which he suffuses his key scenes."[6] Although much of the social comedy in the novel was successfully rendered, Le Fanu wisely followed this more serious vein in the best of his subsequent fiction.

WYLDER'S HAND

All of the most promising elements of Le Fanu's fiction come together in *Wylder's Hand* (1864), with its tightly crafted mystery plot and its hauntingly exquisite prose. The narrator is again Charles de Cresseron, who told the story of *The House by the Churchyard* and now appears in his own right as a minor character in this novel. Charles recalls the events, now many years in the past, when he was called from London to the country village of Gyling-den to assist his cousin, Mark Wylder, in his marriage settlements. The marriage has been arranged as a conven-ience in order to unite two branches of the family for-merly split by ancestral legal vendettas. By marrying his cousin Dorcas, who has inherited Brandon Hall, Mark will bring his considerable fortune to the services of keep-ing the vast estate in the family for future generations. There is no pretense of love between the two, and it soon becomes clear that Mark is smitten with Rachel Lake, their attractive cousin, while Dorcas secretly loves Rach-el's spendthrift brother Stanley.

The mystery plot concerns the disappearance of Mark Wylder shortly before the marriage is to take place. Rachel is absent for a few days at the same time, and the reader is aware that her brother Stanley has in some way impli-cated her in a deeply shameful episode. Letters from Mark Wylder pleading business in London arrive at Brandon Hall, but Mark does not return. Eventually he writes from the Continent, breaking off his engagement to Dor-cas. The final solution to the mystery, with its tragic overtones, is rendered in a powerful dramatic climax to the novel.

Whereas Le Fanu's previous fiction had been set in Ireland, as one would expect, most of the novels and short stories from *Wylder's Hand* onwards are set in England for the most practical of reasons: his London publisher, Richard Bentley, wanted "an English subject in modern times."[7] Since Le Fanu had spent many family holidays in England, he was already provided with English settings that he used brilliantly in his fiction. The town of Gylingden, which appears more than once in his subsequent writing, has been identified as Buxton in Derbyshire, where Le Fanu and his wife stayed soon after their marriage.[8]

In *Wylder's Hand* the setting is powerfully integrated with the characters and events of the novel. The tiny village, with its half-dozen shops, its informal post office, its Hunt Ball—so provincial in comparison with its grander counterparts elsewhere—represents a kind of rural innocence and naiveté against which the drama of evil is enacted. The theme of corruption, engendered by the ancestral rivalries of the Brandons, the Wylders, and the Lakes, is confirmed in the gloomy atmosphere of Brandon Hall, the great house with its wooded grounds, haunted by the ghostlike form of old Uncle Lorne.

The characters in *Wylder's Hand* are among Le Fanu's finest creations. His first compelling women characters—Rachel Lake and Dorcas Brandon—appear in this novel. Unlike the two pretty girls, Lilias and Gertrude, in *The House by the Churchyard*, who remain shadowy figures at best, Rachel and Dorcas come fully alive. Rachel, whose father had squandered the family fortune, maintains a modest independence in a small house on her cousin Dorcas's grounds. The setting, described by the narrator, perfectly represents the spirit of its occupant, even to the fence around the garden symbolically enclosing her in her private world:

> There is, near the Hall, a very pretty glen, called Redman's Dell, very steep, with a stream running at the bottom of it, but so thickly wooded that in summer time you can only now and then catch a glimpse of the water gliding beneath you. Deep in this picturesque ravine, buried among the thick shadows of tall old trees, runs the narrow mill-road, which lower down debouches on the end of the village street. . . . Higher up, on a sort of platform, the steep bank rising high behind it, with its towering old wood overhanging and surrounding . . . stands an old and small two-storied brick and timber house; and though the sun does not very often glimmer on its windows, it yet possesses an air of sad, old-world comfort—a little flower-garden lies in front with a paling round it. But not every kind of flowers will grow there, under the lordly shadow of the elms and chestnuts. (Ch. 7)

The isolated little house, in its deep shadow, with its brave showing of flowers, is Rachel's sanctuary, where she lives with her old nurse Tamar as her only companion.

The invasion of Rachel's sanctuary by her profligate brother Stanley is accompanied by paradisal imagery: Her "little Eden, though overshadowed and encompassed with the solemn sylvan cloister of nature's building, and vocal with sounds of innocence . . . was no more proof than the Mesopotamian haunt of our first parents against the intrusion of darker spirits" (Ch. 7). Stanley does not hesitate to involve his innocent sister in his exploits. Although the precise nature of her tragic involvement in Stanley's bitter feud with Mark Wylder is not disclosed until the end of the novel, it is clear that Rachel thinks of herself as morally tainted.

Before the tragedy Rachel had regarded her garden paling as a protective barrier. Dorcas, commenting on finding young Lord Chelford talking with Rachel over her garden gate, had suggested that he was a suitor: "Suppose, some fine day, he should put his hand over the paling, and take yours, and make you a speech." Rachel conceals her pride with the flippant reply that "peers and princes have quite given over marrying simple maidens of low estate for love and liking," then adds in a tone of mild irony:

> I make a very good nun, Dorcas, as I told Stanley the other day. I sometimes, indeed, receive a male visitor, at the other side of the paling, which is my grille; but to change my way of life is a dream that does not trouble me. (Ch. 13)

When later on, in a moving scene, Chelford does take Rachel's hand over the paling, as Dorcas had predicted, Rachel's renunciation of her own desire as well as his keeps him outside the grille. Chelford does not open the gate and enter; only Stanley, the Satanic force, violates the sanctity of her retreat.

Outwardly unlike her charming and lively cousin Rachel, Dorcas Brandon appears at first to be enigmatically passive. Although she does not love Mark Wylder, Dorcas has acquiesced in the marriage arrangements with regal indifference. Her beauty is overwhelming, as Charles de Cresseron observes when he is first presented to her: "The lady rose, in a soft floating way; tall, black-haired—but a blackness with a dull rich shadow through it. I had only a general impression of large dusky eyes and very exquisite features—more delicate than the Grecian models, and with a wonderful transparency, like tinted marble" (Ch. 2). Charles is fascinated by her apathy. Taking out a miniature of her mother, whom Charles had known, Dorcas gazes at it in a lengthy silence that Charles finds disconcerting. "I suppose she knew I was looking at her," he notes, "but she showed always a queen-like indifference about what people might think or observe." She asks him about the likeness in the miniature, and when he attempts a compliment to her own beauty as different from but equal to that of her mother, she "looked on me for a second or two, with her dark drowsy glance, and then it returned to the picture, which was again in her hand. There was a total want of interest in the careless sort of surprise she vouchsafed my little sally; neither was there the slightest resentment. If a wafer had been stuck upon my forehead, and she had observed it, there might have been just that look and no more" (Ch. 6).

Charles becomes absorbed in the mystery of this woman who was "so indescribably handsome." Still holding the portrait of her mother, Dorcas gives a brief glimpse of hidden emotion, saying to Charles in a low voice: "It is odd how many of our family married for love—wild love-matches. My poor mother was the last. . . .That marrying for love was a fatality in our family. . . .They were all the most beautiful who sacrificed themselves so—they were all unhappy marriages." Knowing that she does not love Mark Wylder, Charles interprets her remarks as an intention to "profit by the errors and misfortunes" of her forebears by marrying without "weakness or passion."

Dorcas is an enigma to others as well. Early in the novel, Rachel, whose residence at Brandon seems to have been of recent date, is still getting to know her. "Dorcas and I are very good friends," she tells Stanley, "but I don't know very well what to make of her. Only I don't think she is quite so dull and apathetic as I at first supposed" (Ch. 8). When Stanley asks if Dorcas is "woman enough to be fussed a little about her marriage," Rachel replies: "Oh, dear, no! she takes the whole affair with a queen-like and supernatural indifference. She is either a fool or a very great philosopher, and there is something grand in the serene obscurity that envelopes her."

As the friendship between the two young women grows to one of mutual trust, Dorcas reveals to Rachel the secret of her violently passionate nature. Showing the jewels given her by Mark, Dorcas tells Rachel that she is sending them back because she cannot marry him. To Rachel's astonishment, Dorcas declares that she is in love with Rachel's brother Stanley Lake, although he is not aware of her feelings. She has struggled in vain against this passion: "I know he's a bad man, a worthless man—selfish, cruel, maybe. Love is not blind with me, but quite insane. . . .I resolved, Rachel, quite to extinguish the madness; but I could not. It was not his doing, nor mine, but something else. There are some families, I think, too wicked for Heaven to protect, and they are given over to the arts of those who hated them in life and pursue them after death" (Ch. 15).

This powerful portrait of a young woman consumed by an irrational and obsessive passion is an unusual one in Victorian fiction. Society's mores dictated that a young lady must endeavor at all costs not to acknowledge, nor even to feel, any interest in a man until he had "spoken" for her hand. Obviously human nature could not always abide by such strictures, but this was regarded as the ideal to which young women should aspire. Dorcas Brandon, with her total disregard for convention, and a deeply passionate nature beneath her regal passivity, is an intriguing psychological study.

The male characters in *Wylder's Hand* are as strongly delineated as the two women. Stanley Lake, with his fair and handsome elegance and his gentlemanly bearing, makes an ingenious villain. Rachel, despite her awareness of his selfish nature, acknowledges in the beginning that he is a "very amusing brother—if not a very cheery or a very useful one" (Ch. 7). Only his "yellow eyes" and his "sly, sleepy smile" give physical signs of his internal corruption. Such is his charm that even when Dorcas finally learns the full extent of his evil, she cannot reject him totally.

Mark Wylder, as coarse and vulgar in manner as Stanley is polished, is equally compelling. He is short and square, with one shoulder higher than the other and a slight hitch when he walks, a broad brown face and small, cunning eyes. Some years at sea have added to his natural swagger. When they meet again at Brandon Hall, Charles de Cresseron is disgusted at the crude manner in which Mark refers to his engagement. "He talked of his fiancée as he might of an opera-girl almost, and was now discussing Miss Lake in the same style" (Ch. 9). To Charles's objections, Mark replies that "the marriage is a sensible sort of thing and I'm determined, of course, to carry it through; but, hang it, a fellow can't help thinking sometimes there are other things besides money, and Dorcas is not my style. Rachel's more that way; she's a *tremendous* [sic] fine girl, by Jove, and a spirited minx too" (Ch. 9). Having admired Mark when they were schoolboys, Charles now analyzes the adult Mark in dispassionate terms:

> Mark had the frankness of callosity, and could recount his evil deeds and confess his vices with hilarity and detail, and was prompt to take his part in a lark, and was a remarkably hard hitter, and never shrank from the brunt of the row; and with these fine qualities, and a much superior knowledge of the ways of the flash world, had commanded my boyish reverence and a general popularity among strangers. But, with all this, he could be as secret as the sea with which he was conversant, and as hard as a stonewall, when it answered his purpose. He had no lack of cunning, and a convenient fund of cool cruelty when that stoical attribute was called for. Years, I dare say, and a

hard life and profligacy, and command, had not made him
less selfish or more humane, or abated his craft and reso-
lution. (Ch. 14)

Sensing trouble brewing between Stanley Lake and Mark
Wylder, Charles remarks that "the manoeuvring and the
ultimate collision of two such generals . . . would be
worth observing" (Ch. 14). Indeed, the confrontation between the two men constitutes the central pivot of the
mystery plot in the novel.

Another corrupting force in *Wylder's Hand* appears in
the character of the lawyer Josiah Larkin. His pretensions
to religious belief and moral propriety deceive the citizens
of Gylingden into regarding him with admiration. Tall
and gaunt, with little ratlike pink eyes, he lies in wait for
opportunities to acquire property—by fair means or
foul—which will fulfill his dream of rising in the social
scale and becoming a landed proprietor. His pretensions
to gentility are delightfully satirized. The narrator notes
that Larkin has an ambition "to pass for a high-bred gentleman, and thought it might be done by a somewhat lofty
and drawling way of talking, and distributing his length
of limb in what he fancied were easy attitudes" (Ch.
5). Larkin is an inveterate name-dropper. He "liked il-
luminating his little narratives, compliments, and reminiscences with plenty of armorial bearings and heraldic
figures, and played out his court-cards in easy and somewhat overpowering profusion" (Ch. 27). Thus he is delighted to be asked to remain for dinner at Brandon Hall,
because "he could henceforward mention, 'the other day,

when I dined at Brandon,' or 'old Lady Chelford assured me, when last I dined at Brandon'" (Ch. 39). Such manifestations, however, are merely external reflections of the evil in Larkin's nature. When he tries to defraud Stanley Lake, the reader sees his dishonesty without generating much indignation; but when he cheats and decieves the good vicar, William Wylder, he becomes despicable.

In the Reverend William Wylder, utterly unlike his brother Mark, Le Fanu gives us an engaging portrait of a genuinely good man. "Slight, gentle, with something of a pale and studious refinement in his face," and an "earnest, sweet smile" (Ch. 3), the vicar is all too easily victimized by Larkin because it never occurs to him to doubt the honesty of his fellow man. The domestic scenes with his homely and loving wife and charming little boy are delicately sketched without cloying sentiment. Although there is no documentary proof, it may be conjectured that the affectionate relations between the father and child may arise from Le Fanu's own experience, since their youngest son was four years old at the time of his wife Susanna's death.

Wylder's Hand is an altogether superb achievement. Its tightly constructed mystery plot matches the best of Wilkie Collins. Its social theme—like that of *The Woman in White*—attacks the greed and cynicism of those who contract marriages for gain among the wealthy and titled classes. The scenes of high drama and the passages of lyric beauty in *Wylder's Hand* are unmatched by any of Le Fanu's contemporaries. He creates in this novel an atmosphere of tragic fatality, a shadowy world in which the two young women can only dream of escape. There is something shimmering, illusory, dreamlike in scenes such as this in which Dorcas addresses her cousin:

> Rachel, dear, I have a plan for you and me: we shall be old maids, you and I, and live together like the ladies of Llangollen; . . . and with the winter's snow we'll vanish from Brandon, and appear with the early flowers at our cottage among the beautiful woods and hills of Wales. Will you come, Rachel? (Ch. 24)

The same spirit pervades the scene in Venice where Charles sees the two young women: "The gondola which bore the musicians floated by—a slender hand over the gunwale trailed its fingers in the water. Unseen I saw. Rachel and Dorcas, beautiful in the sad moonlight, passed so near we could have spoken—passed me like spirits—never more, it may be, to cross my sight in life" (Ch. 24).

UNCLE SILAS

Le Fanu was at the peak of his powers in 1864, the year which saw not only the publication of *Wylder's Hand* in book form but the second of his two finest novels, *Uncle Silas: A Story of Bartram-Haugh*. Less a mystery story than a Gothic tale of terror, *Uncle Silas* is a superb example of the literary form begun by Horace Walpole in *The Castle of Otranto* (1764), developed by Ann Radclyffe in *The Mysteries of Udolpho* (1794), and perpetuated today in the popular form of the Gothic romance. Using many of the traditional elements such as the isolated mansion and the heroine threatened by evil forces, Le Fanu raises them to the level of first-rate fiction.

Novels that dealt with murder and violent crime, with or without Gothic elements, were often attacked by reviewers, and Le Fanu had come in for a share of criticism for his use of such elements in *The House by the Churchyard* and *Wylder's Hand*. In company with Dickens, Collins, Charles Reade, Mary Elizabeth Braddon, and other contemporaries, Le Fanu resented the label "sensation novelist," and in a preface to the three-volume edition of *Uncle Silas* he attempted to defend his work on the ground that Sir Walter Scott used the same devices. May the "writer of this Tale," he asks,

> be permitted a few words of remonstrance against the promiscuous application of the term "sensation," to that large school of fiction which transgresses no one of those canons of construction and morality which, in producing the unapproachable "Waverley Novels," their great author imposed upon himself? No one, it is assumed, would describe Sir Walter Scott's romances as "sensation novels;" yet in that marvellous series there is not a single tale in which death, crime, and in some form, mystery, have not a place.

There is some justice in this claim. Le Fanu might have said the same of Shakespeare, as others have done. Perhaps the only reply is that the greater the artist, the more he is ultimately read for qualities other than those of sensation. On such a scale, Le Fanu's best work is well worth reading on its own merits, whether or not it deals in sensational themes.

Le Fanu had used the plot of Uncle Silas in two earlier versions, as he explains in the preface. What he calls "a leading situation" in *Uncle Silas* was used in an early story "A Passage in the Secret History of an Irish Countess," which had appeared in the *Dublin University Magazine* in 1839, and again in "The Murdered Cousin," one of the short stories of 1851. Since the earlier stories were published anonymously in Ireland, he believes it "unlikely that any of his readers should have encountered, and still more so that they should remember, this trifle." He modestly mentions it now "lest he should be charged with plagiarism—always a disrespect to a reader." In this instance, the early versions are less effective than the final novel. Names, settings, and events are all altered. The story of the Irish Countess, set in eighteenth-century Ireland, was updated and set in Derbyshire in *Uncle Silas*, in accordance with his publisher's desire for "an English setting in modern times." The intermediate version, in which the cousin was the victim, as the title implies, was happily changed. Neither of the short stories contains the rich development of character and incident achieved in the novel. Le Fanu was able to sustain the high quality of invention throughout the three-volume length of *Uncle Silas*, whereas later on, as noted above, he worked best in the shorter form.

Le Fanu's unique accomplishment in *Uncle Silas* is the creation of genuine terror. The heroine, a sheltered girl of seventeen when the story opens, is gradually drawn into a net of danger which becomes all the more appalling because the circumstances seem so deceptively innocent. Le Fanu builds the pressure by alternating between states of safety and of menace. Again and again, a threat of danger is countered by an apparent release. Because the events grow naturally out of character and circumstance, unlike the often contrived terrors of the traditional Gothic tale, the reader is swept along toward a grand finale of horror in the chapter entitled "The Hour of Death."

The character of Uncle Silas is brilliantly devised. When the novel first appeared as a serial in the *Dublin University Magazine* its title was *Maud Ruthyn*, the name of the heroine. The change of title for the book edition was auspicious, bringing the focus as it does upon the wonderfully enigmatic figure of Maud's uncle, as Le Fanu manipulates the contradictory versions of his character. Since Maud does not actually meet her uncle until the half-way point in the novel, the title affirms the importance of her fascination with her mysterious relative. From childhood she has admired the portrait of Silas that hangs in the oak room at Knowl:

> It was a full-length, and represented a singularly handsome young man, dark, slender, elegant, in a costume then quite obsolete, though I believe it was seen at the beginning of this century—white leather pantaloons and top-boots, a buff waistcoat, and a chocolate-coloured coat, and the hair long and brushed back.
>
> There was a remarkable elegance and a delicacy in the features, but also a character of resolution and ability that quite took the portrait out of the category of mere fops or fine men. When people looked at it for the first time, I

have so often heard the exclamation—"What a wonderfully handsome man!" and then, "What a clever face!" (Ch. 2)

Maud's taciturn father, Austin Ruthyn, rarely speaks of his brother. In answer to her childish question about why he is "always so sad about Uncle Silas," he replies: "Your uncle is a man of great talents, great faults, and great wrongs. His talents have not availed him; his faults are long ago repented of; and his wrongs I believe he feels less than I do, but they are deep" (Ch. 12).

Later, Maud learns from her cousin, Lady Monica Knollys, that Silas as a young man had been an inveterate gambler, whose debts were paid repeatedly by his elder brother; but when Silas married a socially unacceptable woman, his brother, in true Victorian fashion, broke off all relations with him. Oddly enough, adds Monica, he relented "on the very occasion which some people said ought to have totally separated them"—the circumstance that Silas was suspected of having committed a murder. Although Austin no longer gave Silas money nor visited him, he was adamant in declaring him innocent of the crime, and Maud passionately agrees. Now at the age of seventeen, she romanticizes the enigmatic face of the portrait: "There stood the roué—the duellist—and, with all his faults, the hero too! . . . Some day it might come to pass that I, girl as I was, might contribute by word or deed towards the vindication of that long-suffering, gallant, and romantic prodigal" (Ch. 13).

The details of the murder of which Silas was accused

constitute an early use of the locked-room formula. A Mr. Charke, to whom Silas owed enormous sums of money, was found with his throat cut in a room in Silas's house, with the doors and windows securely locked. Thorough investigation proved fruitless and a verdict of suicide was brought in. In the end, the solution of this mystery forms a part of the grand climax of the novel.

When by the terms of her father's will Maud becomes her uncle's ward, the distrust expressed by her friends conflicts with her own loyalty to her uncle. Her first meeting with Silas leaves her uncertain but hopeful. He had "a face like marble, with a fearful monumental look, and, for an old man, singularly vivid strange eyes. . . . His eyebrows were still black, though his hair descended from his temples in long locks of the purest silver and fine as silk, nearly to his shoulders." She is bewildered by his gaze upon her—"was it derision, or anguish, or cruelty, or patience?" (Ch. 23) His formal courtesy, his assurances of affection, and his permission for Maud and her cousin Milly to roam about freely, are all reassuring, yet she notes Milly's fear of him. Was he "martyr, angel, demon"? Uncle Silas's polished conversation, laced with French phrases and bits of poetry, contains sudden flashes of animosity. And so the pattern is set for the alteration of Maud's confidence and fear.

The figure of Dr. Bryerly, the Swedenborgian friend of Maud's father, at first presents a similar ambiguity for Maud. When she was a small child, soon after her mother's death, he frightened her by describing the visions of an afterworld inhabited by her mother. Again, after her father's death, she finds his unorthodox rituals disturbing. At Austin's coffin he says, "I must look on the face as I pray. He is in his place; I here on earth. He in the spirit: I in the flesh. The neutral ground lies there. So are carried the vibrations, and so the light of earth and heaven reflected back and forward—apaugasma, a wonderful though helpless engine." Later on Maud learns to trust in Bryerly's goodness, despite his curious beliefs and practices. Le Fanu's own interest in Swedenborgian theory, more explicit in this novel than elsewhere, is handled with an odd tentativeness. Whether he feared alienating his readers by appearing to proselytize, or whether he himself was only a partial devotee, it is impossible to determine. Perhaps, like Maud's father, who sent her to the Church of England service but did not attend himself, Le Fanu's interest in religions was that of a scholar, not a believer. Yet other passages in his fiction affirm both Swedenborgian visions and conventional attitudes toward belief. Certainly the character of Dr. Bryerly is odd but virtuous.

Uncle Silas is a novel of contrasts. There are not one but two grand houses, Knowl and Bartram-Haugh, both estates of the Ruthyn family. The quiet elegance of Knowl, where Maud has grown up in peaceful security, contrasts with the neglected grandeur of Bartram-Haugh, with its ambiguous air of innocence and deception. The two halves of the novel divide at the point of Maud's entrance into Bartram. Le Fanu makes superb use of a mirrorlike effect, as the events at Bartram appear like distorted images of Maud's former life at Knowl. This is especially true of the ominous reappearance of characters who seemed at first only trivial. In the early scenes, the grotesque governess, Madame de la Rougierre, with her affectations and caprices, was merely irritating to Maud, who was delighted at her dismissal. When Madame reappears in the second half of the novel, she becomes a wholly sinister figure. Similarly, at Knowl, Dudley Ruthyn—whose identity was at that time unknown to Maud—was merely a nuisance in his attempts to pursue her. At Bartram, the oafish Dudley becomes a brutal and threatening force.

A number of parallels exist between *Uncle Silas* and Wilkie Collins's *The Woman in White*. The two great houses in *Uncle Silas* reflect the contrasting houses of Limmeridge—where Laura Fairlie grew up sheltered and secure—and Blackwater Park—which for all its deceptive everyday appearance was the scene of danger. Both heroines are the potential victims of those who have absolute legal power over their persons as well as their fortunes. Their natural protectors, in each case, are unable to intervene: like Marian Halcombe and Walter Hartright in *The Woman in White*, cousin Monica and Dr. Bryerly are powerless to avert the potential threat to Maud in *Uncle Silas*. Other echoes are unmistakable. The invalid hypochondriac Uncle Silas owes some of his characteristics to Laura's uncle, Frederick Fairlie, even to his abhorrence of noise. Madame de la Rougierre bears some resemblance to Madame Fosco. Both are sinister "foreign" women (Madame Fosco is in fact English but has become more Italianate than her husband), and both treat the heroines with hypocritical fondness while plotting against them.

Except for the locked room subplot, *Uncle Silas* is not

essentially a mystery story like *The Woman in White* or Le Fanu's own *Wylder's Hand.* The pattern is one of sheer suspense. Even though the first-person narration of Maud herself assures her ultimate survival, the reader is gripped by the working out of the impending peril and the fascination of the characters and circumstances which bring it about. In his subsequent fiction, Le Fanu never again matched the achievement of this splendid novel.

Le Fanu's next novel, *Guy Deverell* (1865), lacks the power of its predecessors but is still worth reading today. Again, an old crime from the past is the focus of the plot, as it was in *The House by the Churchyard* and to some degree in *Uncle Silas.* Family feuds and a theme of revenge provide the background for the group of idle rich who gather at Sir Jekyl Marlowe's country mansion. Some twenty-five years earlier, Sir Jekyl had killed his rival, Guy Deverell, in a duel. Deverell's friend Varbarrière, who was present at the duel, regarded it as nothing short of murder and now, disguised as a mysterious Mr. Strangways, he brings Guy's son and namesake to England to gain revenge. When young Guy Deverell and Sir Jekyl's daughter Beatrix fall in love, they unwittingly become a Romeo and Juliet upon whom Le Fanu eventually bestows a happy ending.

A tone of sophistication appears in this novel, with its worldly men and women engaging in flirtations, and its serious theme of adultery. Sir Jekyl, far from a stock villain, is described with devastating crispness: "Beatrix was fond of her father, who was really a good-natured man, in the common acceptance of the term, that is to say, he had high animal spirits, and liked to see people pleasant about him, and was probably as kind as a tolerably selfish and vicious man can be." Beatrix and the young Guy Deverell, ostensibly hero and heroine, tend to fade into the background for much of the novel, as Le Fanu becomes absorbed in the moral drama he is creating. The beautiful and passionate Lady Jane Lennox, whose affair with Sir Jekyl generates tragic consequences, becomes the dominant figure. Sir Jekyl's death from the wounds received in a duel with Lady Jane's elderly husband completes the formal pattern of revenge in the novel, with its condemnation of artificial social values.

Although he introduces such Gothic conventions as secret passages and mysterious rooms in the mansion at Marlowe, Le Fanu's impulse in *Guy Deverell* is to move away from fiction of horror and suspense and into a study of contemporary society. One has the feeling that he wanted to move in a new direction in his fiction but feared losing the readers who expected a thriller from his pen.

Certainly Le Fanu's next novel, *All in the Dark* (1866), departs from the tale of terror, marking a return to the mode of social comedy with which he had experimented in *The House by the Churchyard*. The vein of social satire emerging in *Guy Deverell* also appears in *All in the Dark*, in which spiritualism is lightly spoofed and social pretensions are exposed. A Victorian love story provides the central focus of the plot. William Maubray, the ward of his Aunt Dinah Perfect, grew up at Gilroyd Hall, where his cousin Violet Darkwell had often visited as a child. Their romance, hampered by each believing the other is engaged to someone else, is saved from mediocrity by the delicate charm with which Le Fanu invariably presents young lovers. Violet is unimpressed by her suitor, the local squire, Vane Trevor, despite his assumption that he has only to ask to be accepted. Le Fanu deftly satirizes the squire's reflections on learning that Violet's father is a barrister in London and has some sons:

> Trevor sighed. He was thinking what low fellows these sons might possibly be. A barrister. He remembered young Boles's father visiting Rugby once, a barrister, making fifteen hundred a year, a shabby, lean-looking fellow, with a stoop, and a seedy black frock coat, and grizzled whiskers, who talked in a sharp, dry way, with sometimes a little brow-beating tendency—not a bit like a gentleman. On the other hand, to be sure, there were lots of swells among them; but still there was the image of old Boles's father intruding into the moonlight, and poking about the old trees of Gilroyd.

Social pretensions of the opposite kind are amusingly treated in the efforts of Mrs. Kincton Knox to secure William for her daughter Clara in the mistaken belief that he is his cousin and heir to a title.

The gentle satire of Aunt Dinah and her spiritualism may seem surprising from an author who was deeply immersed in the visions of Swedenborgianism. If even a supreme rationalist like Arthur Conan Doyle could become a devotee of spiritualism, one would expect Le Fanu to have at least some predisposition toward belief in "the spirit world," but he evidently regarded the whole appa-

ratus of table-rapping and speaking spirits as childish ab-
surdity. Aunt Dinah is presented as lovable but credulous.
Le Fanu gives William a whole series of pseudo–ghost experiences, perhaps intended to satisfy his readers' taste for
terrors, and then explains them away as sleepwalking.

Le Fanu's excursion into domestic comedy in *All in the
Dark* was not poular with the public, a problem which
he discusses in a letter to his publisher Bentley: "I am
half sorry I wrote 'All in the Dark' with my own name to
it. I am now convinced it is a great disadvantage to give
the public something quite different from what your an-
tecedents had led them to expect from you."[9] He nevertheless pursued his own course in much of his subsequent
fiction.

Of Le Fanu's works published after 1866, only the
novel *Checkmate* (1871) and a long story, "The Room in
the Dragon Volant," are of particular interest to readers
of mystery fiction. *The Tenants of Malory* (1867), and *A
Lost Name* (1868), a much-extended version of "The Evil
Guest," are uninspired. More readable are *Haunted Lives*
(1868) and *The Rose and the Key* (1871), with their lively
heroines, both wealthy girls who elect to assert some independence in their lives. *Haunted Lives* contains some
deeply moving moments, and *The Rose and the Key* comes
close to *Uncle Silas* in the creation of horror in the scenes
at the insane asylum. *The Wyvern Mystery* (1869), despite
its promising title, is the least rewarding of the group,
straining the reader's credulity with improbabilities and
unmotivated actions. *Morley Court* (1873) is merely a re-
print of the early *Cock and the Anchor*, and the last novel,

ironically entitled *Willing to Die* (1873) and written during Le Fanu's last illness, has little to recommend it.

Checkmate makes use of the theme by now familiar in Le Fanu's fiction of an old crime that has never been solved. A brother of the Arden family was murdered twenty years or so ago, naming his attacker as Yelland Mace, but Mace has disappeared without trace. A gentleman of enormous wealth, Walter Longcluse, who has become an acquaintance of the family, startles the old housekeeper who had witnessed the murder, although Loncluse bears no resemblance whatever to Mace. The theme of the profligate brother's exploitation of the innocent sister, reminiscent of Stanley and Rachel Lake in *Wylder's Hand*, is used again in the relationship of Richard and Alice Arden. Early in the novel a murder is committed at a gambling house, in which Longcluse is mysteriously involved. An ex-detective of the London Police, who has been dismissed for "a piece of over-cleverness" (never defined), obtains a boot worn by Longcluse on the night of the murder. Alice Arden is imprisoned in her own house and makes a dramatic escape with the aid of a courageous servant girl. The good uncle, David Arden, engages in some amateur detective work and traces the doctor in Paris who had performed plastic surgery on the murderer, undoubtedly the first use of that device in mystery fiction. Such are the ingredients of this interesting but flawed novel. Despite its weaknesses—some padding and repetition, some diffuseness where tight construction would be welcome—*Checkmate* offers lively reading and ends like a modern mystery story with a detailed explanation of the steps that led up to the final solution.

"The Room in the Dragon Volant," the only one of the five tales in the collection *In a Glass Darkly* (1872) that is not a ghost story, neatly combines Gothic horror with some aspects of the mystery story. George Becket, a young Englishman traveling to Paris, is easily enticed by a beautiful woman into nearly losing not only a small fortune but his life as well. There is a dramatic scene at a masked ball with a mysterious palanquin; there is a detective, Colonel Gaillarde of the French police, whom the young man mistakes for his enemy; there is a secret passage at the inn; and finally there is a climax of horror worthy of Poe in which the hero, drugged with "Mortis Imago," helplessly hears the plot to bury him alive in the Parisian cemetery of Père la Chaise. All of this apparent nonsense is transformed in the telling by Le Fanu's deft handling of the first-person narration. Young Becket's disingenuous account of his experience creates a pleasant dramatic irony in which the reader perceives more than the naive narrator, at the same time finding him engagingly sympathetic, while the story expertly builds to its dramatic ending.

Dorothy Sayers once described Le Fanu as "melodramatic, but a writer of real literary attainment, and gifted with a sombre power which has seldom been equalled in painting the ghastly and the macabre."[10] While Le Fanu never captured the immense readerships of Dickens or Collins, his was nevertheless a known and respected name, and his best works are among the chief ornaments of Victorian suspense fiction.

5

Some Minor Voices

The three authors treated in this chapter represent what was happening in mystery fiction between 1860 and 1890—in other words, between *The Woman in White* and Sherlock Holmes. The two British authors, Mary Elizabeth Braddon and James Payn, followed Wilkie Collins in writing social novels which often, but not always, contained elements of mystery and crime, whereas the American author, Anna Katharine Green, devoted herself exclusively to a recognizable mystery formula in all of her fiction, anticipating Conan Doyle by almost a decade. During this period, a whole crop of minor British writers appeared in the crime-and-detection field, including such names as Mrs. Henry Wood, Andrew Forrester, Florence Warden, Charles Gibbons, Arthur Griffith, Hawley Smart, H. F. Wood, and Fergus Hume. None of these, however, matched the quality of Mary Braddon's fiction nor that of James Payn at his best; and no account of this period would be complete without recognizing the contribution of

Anna Katharine Green, the first American Agatha Christie.

MARY ELIZABETH BRADDON

If we had to rely solely upon the information about Mary Braddon given in the *Dictionary of National Biography*, we would have a limited view of the life of this lively author. Except for her birthdate, incorrectly given as 1837 instead of 1835, the article is accurate as far as it goes. According to the *DNB*, Mary Braddon was "The youngest daughter of Henry Braddon, solicitor and author of several works on sporting subjects, a member of an old Cornish family, of Skisdon Lodge, St. Kew, Cornwall, by his wife, Fanny, daughter of J. White, of county Cavan." After receiving a "good private education," she published two novels and some poems before achieving her first success with *Lady Audley's Secret* in 1862. In 1874 she married the publisher John Maxwell, was the mother of five children, edited several magazines, and published some eighty novels before her death in 1915. Written by the literary critic and bibliographer Michael Sadleir, the article warmly praises her fiction but maintains a discreet silence about the thornier aspects of her life.

The excellent recent biography by Robert Lee Wolff, *Sensational Victorian: The Life and Fiction of Mary Elizabeth Braddon,*[1] reveals Mary Braddon as a forthright woman who refused to accept the role of helpless female dictated by Victorian society. Her real story reads like one of her own "sensation" novels. Her father, the solicitor, was in fact a handsome reprobate who rarely practiced law and only fitfully supported his wife and three children, finally deserting them and leaving his wife to manage on a very small and erratic income. Mary's much older sister and brother each eventually settled abroad. Her sister Maggie married an Italian and went to live in Naples; her brother Edward went to India and later to Tasmania, where he became Prime Minister in 1894.

Meanwhile, Mary and her mother survived as best they could. When there was money, Mary went to school or had a governess; otherwise she had lessons with her mother, which for the most part she enjoyed. In a fragment of memoir that she began to write in the year before her death, Mary records that her mother "never treated me as a child . . . but talked with me as if I were on the same plane," and her formal teaching, never onerous, was spiced with Mrs. Braddon's Irish wit and humor.[2] Mary remembered delightful childhood visits to Skisdon, the family estate in Cornwall, but for the most part she and her mother lived in London, often on the very edge of poverty. That Mary felt bitterness toward her father is evident both in her letters and in her fiction, where charming ne'er-do-well fathers are likely to be treated with scorn.

No simpering Victorian heroine, Mary decided at the age of twenty that she was tired of genteel poverty and would earn money for her mother and herself by going on the stage. Her memoir records that for a young girl of good family to enter acting at that time was "a thing to be spoken of with bated breath, the lapse of a lost soul," and that it "convulsed her family to the most distant cousin."[3]

Accompanied by her mother, who was apparently willing to acquiesce in her daughter's adventure, Mary played for three years in the provinces and in London as "Mary Seyton." Rarely the ingenue, she played character roles which seemed to suit her strong personality. When she left the stage to turn to writing, she met with financial success beyond her wildest hopes but never forgot her experiences in the theater and often described them in her fiction.

Probably some time in 1860 Mary Braddon met John Maxwell, an Irishman who had lived in London since his youth and who was involved in publishing ventures. Although he had a wife living in a mental asylum in Dublin, he and Mary became lovers and had five children in the years between 1862 and 1868. The social stigma of living out of wedlock created some painful episodes, at least one of which was brought on in 1864 by John Maxwell's ill-advised notice in several London newspapers of their "marriage." Perhaps Mary's fame as an author had made it more difficult to conceal their illicit relationship than would have been possible for an unknown couple. Whatever the reasons, the public statement was instantly denied by the brother-in-law of the tragically ill Mrs. Maxwell, creating a scandal the publicity of which could probably have been avoided.

Meanwhile, Mary Braddon and John Maxwell lived together as man and wife, maintaining a home for her mother and for his five children as well as the surviving four of their own, until the death of his wife in 1874 made it possible for them to marry. All of the children were extremely fond of Mary, whose energy must have been prodigious. Writing an average of two novels a year and editing magazines, she yet managed to be a warm and affectionate mother to her large brood. Her son, the novelist W. B. Maxwell, describes in his own autobiography how his mother "got through her immense amount of work as if by magic. She never seemed to be given any time in which to do it. She had no stated hours, no part of the day to be held secure from disturbances and intrusions. She was never inaccessible. Everybody went uninvited to her library, we children, the servants, importunate visitors."[4] With her Irish wit and fun-loving nature, Mary, like her own mother, was a delightful companion.

Success came early to Mary Braddon. After two apprentice novels and some verse, she produced an overnight bestseller in *Lady Audley's Secret*. Written originally to help John Maxwell launch a new magazine in 1861, a venture that lasted for only twelve issues, the novel appeared a few months later in another journal and was picked up by the new publishing firm of Tinsley Brothers, whose three-volume *Lady Audley* in 1862 brought instant fortune to both author and publishers. Frankly aiming for the market created by Wilkie Collins's *The Woman in White*, Mary Braddon succeeded so well that, despite the popularity of all her subsequent work, she was best known as the author of *Lady Audley's Secret*, the novel she had written in great haste at the age of twenty-six. The money continued to pour in, as she turned out two or more novels each year. In 1864 John Maxwell's own publishing company started bringing out her work, thus keeping all the profits in the family, as it were. By 1866 they were able to acquire Lichfield, a handsome Georgian house in Richmond, Surrey, where they resided for the remainder of their lives.

As a "sensation" novelist, Mary Braddon was assailed by those critics who found stories of crime immoral and tainted. As in similar attacks upon Wilkie Collins, the chief complaint was that "an authoress of originality and merit," as one critic described her, ought to aspire to higher things. By "making the literature of the Kitchen the favourite reading of the Drawing room," she was betraying social propriety. Exasperating as were such attacks, Mary Braddon herself was more concerned that the speed with which she wrote did not allow for the development of excellence. In her long correspondence with her literary mentor, novelist Bulwer Lytton, she was often apologetic about her own merits. "It has been my good, or bad, fortune," she wrote, "to be flung into a very rapid market, & to have everything printed and published almost before the ink with which it was written was dry." But she doubted that she had the proper incentive to strive for great art, for she "learned to look at everything in a mercantile sense, and to write solely for the circulating library reader."[5]

Within her self-imposed limitations, however, Mary Braddon's fiction is the product of a highly intelligent and cultured woman whose amusing and sometimes cynical view of life adds spice to her work. Like Wilkie Collins and Sheridan Le Fanu, she moved away from the "sensation" novel in much of her later work, turning to historical novels and to purely social themes, often derived from her interest in Balzac and Zola. However, the quality of her fiction in later years did not decline as dramatically as that of Collins and Le Fanu. After the 1880s the throb of life is milder but the writing remains vigorous to the end. At the time of her death in 1915, she was still a widely read and much admired literary figure.

Mary Braddon's novels were special favorites of many of her distinguished contemporaries. Arnold Bennett described her as "part of England."[6] Her work was admired by Collins, Reade, Bulwer, and even the fastidious Henry James, who had written an admiring review of her work in 1865, when he was a precocious twenty-one, and who became her friend in later years. Robert Louis Stevenson wrote to her from Samoa that he wished his "days to be bound each to each by Miss Braddon's novels." Tennyson declared that he was "simply steeped in Miss Braddon," and Gladstone praised her "facility and skill."[7]

Gratifying as were such tributes, Mary Braddon would perhaps have been more deeply touched by one she never saw, an entry about her which Charles Reade made in his personal notebook in 1874: "I don't know where to find a better woman. Industrious, self-denying, gentle, affectionate, talented and utterly unassuming, a devoted daughter, faithful wife, loving mother, and kindly stepmother."[8]

In *Lady Audley's Secret* Mary Braddon took to the new Wilkie Collins formula like a duck to water. The only weakness in the plot occurs in the opening sequences, in which we are asked to believe that George Talboys left his adored wife and infant son to go to Australia, that for nearly four years he did not write to her, and that he amassed twenty thousand pounds in gold which he carried home in his pockets, planning to surprise his dear little wife. After this unpromising beginning, however, the events of the ensuing mystery are expertly devised. George learns that his wife has changed her name and become Lady Audley, the wife of an older man with both money and a title. When he visits her at her country home, the two are seen walking in the garden, after which George Talboys disappears. Has Lady Audley murdered him in order to preserve her secret from her husband, or has George Talboys gone abroad (as she claims)? The reader is lured on with a series of revelations about Lady Audley's past, and the novel culminates in some fine dramatic scenes and some surprise twists which forecast the formulas of twentieth-century mystery fiction. Even Lady Audley's "secret" is not what the reader is initially led to expect.

As in Collins's *The Woman in White*, the detecting is done in *Lady Audley's Secret* by the hero rather than by professionals. Sir Michael's nephew, Robert Audley, who has heretofore been a lazy and self-indulgent bachelor, is stirred by the disappearance of his friend George Talboys to exert himself to solve the mystery. When Lady Audley scornfully tells him that he "ought to have been a detective-police officer," he replies that he thinks he might have been a good one because he is patient (Ch. 18). Robert is glad that, although he is a barrister, he was never ambitious enough to become a Queen's Counsel, for "if I were a distinguished Q.C., I could not do this sort of thing. . . . My time would be worth a guinea or so a minute," whereas now he is free to pursue his detection. Not only does he unravel the mystery through his investigations, he also finds unsuspected personal strength in this first challenge of his erstwhile indolent life.

In this early novel Mary Braddon shows the talent for deft characterization that never deserted her throughout her writing career. Even minor characters are sharply sketched. George's unfeeling father, Harcourt Talboys, "was like his own square-built, northern-fronted, shelterless house. There were no shady nooks in his character into which one could creep for shelter from his hard daylight. . . . There were no curves in his character—his mind ran in straight lines, never diverging to the right or the left to round off their pitiless angles" (Ch. 22). The schoolmistress, Miss Tonks, was "wintry and rather frost-bitten in aspect, and seemed to bring cold air in the scanty folds of her somber merino dress. She was no age in particular, and looked as if she had never been younger, and would never grow older, but would remain forever working backward and forward in her narrow groove, like some self-feeding machine for the instruction of young ladies" (Ch. 26). If there is an echo of Dickens here, there is also the strong stamp of Mary Braddon's own idiom.

The major characters are powerfully drawn: Sir Michael Audley, madly in love at the age of fifty-five with his childlike wife; his daughter Alicia, with her love of horses and outdoor life; and Lady Audley herself, with her golden ringlets, her clinging sweetness, and her enchanting blue eyes—all are strongly developed characters. The events of the novel may be melodramatic, in keeping with the demands of the sensation market, but the characters are far more fully realized than those of conventional melodrama. Like Wilkie Collins, Mary Braddon gives us not merely a suspenseful plot but an often penetrating view of Victorian society.

A few examples from among Mary Braddon's more than eighty novels will give some indication of the nature of her mystery fiction. Of the novels published in the first years after *Lady Audley's Secret*, one of the most entertaining is *Henry Dunbar* (1864). In his youth, Henry Dunbar was banished to India by his father for having engaged in shady transactions in their London banking firm. An employee, Joseph Wilmot, who had aided Henry, served a prison term for his part in the affair. On the death of his father some twenty-five years later, Henry returns to England to take over the firm and is met by Wilmot, now bent on revenge. When Wilmot's body is found in a wood where the two men had walked together, Henry is briefly suspected of the murder, but with no evidence against him he returns to his estate and leads the life of a wealthy country gentleman. With some ingenious twists and deft manipulation of clues, the suspense of the murder plot is well sustained. In his memoir, Mary Braddon's son recalls his youthful pleasure in reading his mother's novels, mentioning the "tremor of excitement" he felt on reading *Henry Dunbar*, and his gratitude to his elder sister for not disclosing the plot.⁹

The detecting in *Henry Dunbar* is at first assumed by the young hero, Clement Austin, who is in love with Wilmot's daughter. Clement eventually realizes that his amateur efforts are insufficient and goes to Scotland Yard for help. Henry Carter, the detective assigned to the case, is briskly efficient in the tradition of Inspector Bucket of *Bleak House* and the detectives of the popular casebooks of the period, but he is less attractive than Collins's Sergeant Cuff, who had not yet appeared on the fictional scene. Clement is not at first impressed by Carter: he is "a businesslike-looking man, short and stoutly built, with close-cropped hair, very little shirt-collar, a shabby black satin stock, and a coat buttoned tightly across the chest. He was a man whose appearance was something between the aspect of a shabby-genteel half-pay captain and an unlucky stockbroker." Nevertheless, despite his rather dubious appearance, Clement "liked the steady light of his small grey eyes, and the decided expression of his thin lips and prominent chin" (Ch. 37). Carter tolerantly permits Clement to tag along in the investigation, provided he is willing to act under orders. Clement is delighted with Carter's "enthusiastic love of his profession" and becomes an admiring Watson as he describes Carter's methods in tracking down clues, examining evidence, and using mild deception to elicit information. In the closing chapters there are some splendid scenes of chase before the end is reached.

Mary Braddon would not have been a popular Victorian

novelist if she had not engaged in a certain amount of sentimentality in her fiction. One cannot refrain from suspecting that she wrote many such passages with tongue firmly in cheek, especially when characters engage in excessive degrees of noble self-sacrifice. In *Henry Dunbar* the heroine Margaret persists in rejecting the faithful Clement because she feels tainted by her father's past, until at last love prevails in the conventional happy ending. Sentimentality of every kind was meat and drink to the circulating library audience, and while Braddon gave them plenty of sustenance, she could not refrain from flashes of pithy commentary from time to time. In one such passage in *Henry Dunbar*, she discusses the superiority of love based upon growing esteem as opposed to love at first sight with a pretty face. Othello, she says, "loved Desdemona because she was pretty, and looked at him with sweet maidenly glances of pity when he told her those prosy stories of his." He loved her "because he admired her, and not because he knew her; and so, by and bye, on the strength of a few foul hints from a scoundrel, he is ready to believe this gentle, pitiful girl the basest and most abandoned of women" (Ch. 20). Hamlet would never have made this mistake:

> Hamlet would not so have acted had it been his fate to marry the woman he loved. Depend upon it, the Danish prince had watched Ophelia closely, and knew all the ins and outs of that young lady's temper, and had laid conversational traps for her occasionally, I dare say, trying to entice her into some bit of toadyism that should betray any

latent taint of falsehood inherited from poor time-serving Polonius. The Prince of Denmark would have been rather a fidgety husband, perhaps, but he would never have had recourse to a murderous bolster at the instigation of a low-born knave. (Ch. 20)

Such amusing expressions of Braddon's characteristically down-to-earth philosophy do much to counteract the high-flown sentiment in the more conventional passages of her fiction.

A pair of novels—*Birds of Prey* (1867) and its sequel, *Charlotte's Inheritance* (1868)—were popular examples of Mary Braddon's mystery fiction. The formula is not who-dunit but how to expose the culprit and how to prevent another murder. *Birds of Prey* opens with Philip Seldon poisoning his best friend in order to marry the wealthy widow; *Charlotte's Inheritance* concludes with his protracted attempt to murder his stepdaughter, whom Seldon has secretly learned is the heiress of an even larger fortune. The theme of lost heirs dominates both novels. The detection, chiefly carried on by the young hero with the unlikely name Valentine Hawkehurst, is not directly connected with uncovering the murder but with the extensive searches for the heirs of one Matthew Haygarth, who died intestate. Echoes of *The Woman in White* are evident in the emphasis upon records found in parish registers and in the rambling conversations of the "oldest inhabitants" who might have knowledge of Haygarth's descendants. In the end, not one but two lost heirs are discovered and the estate is sorted out to everyone's satisfaction.

A certain amount of artificial contrivance occurs in the course of the six volumes of this pair of novels. Early on, *Charlotte's Inheritance* severely strains the reader's credulity when a dying young woman is so ill that she "forgets" to tell her sister that she has married and had a son. Coincidences abound in order to bring certain characters together. Apart from such obvious deficiencies, however, the novels have considerable merit. In addition to the usual cast of well-defined characters, there is social commentary on the dependence of women in Victorian society. Diana Paget, one of the two heroines, has led a precarious existence with her father, a gambler and a con artist who regards her as a burden and an inconvenience. When she finally finds a home with friends as an unpaid companion, Valentine pities her, reflecting that he himself "could go out into the world, and cut his way through the forest of difficulty with the axe of the conqueror. But what could a woman do who found herself in the midst of that dismal forest?" He cries out to himself a protest that would have been shocking in the 1860s: "O! let us have women doctors, women lawyers, women parsons, women stone-breakers—anything rather than these dependent creatures who sit in other people's houses working prie-dieu chairs and pining for freedom" (*Birds of Prey*, Book VI, Ch. 1).

Diana's scorn of her father, a recurring theme in Braddon's fiction, reflects the author's own resentment toward the father who had failed to provide for her or to earn her admiration. In the novel, Diana had lived with her father; "she had tasted the bitterness of dependence upon him—

ten times more bitter than dependence upon strangers. She had shown him her threadbare garments day after day, and had pleaded for a little money, to be put off with a lying excuse" (*Charlotte's Inheritance*, Book III, Ch. 4). She could cheerfully have endured poverty with an honest and loving father; what she could not forgive was that he gave her no affection and was too despicable to deserve her respect. Without the alternative of earning her own living, she must remain dependent upon others. Only a young woman with the extraordinary fortitude of Mary Braddon herself could break out of the pattern.

A final example of Mary Braddon's fiction, *A Strange World* (1875), published in the second decade of her long writing career, contains a tightly constructed murder plot. Again, the formula is not that of the whodunit, for the reader is aware from the beginning that Churchill Penwyn has murdered his young cousin James Penwyn in order to inherit the lucrative family estate in Cornwall. The suspense lies in how the disclosure will come about.

The opening scenes in a provincial theater give some amusing glimpses into the realities of stage life, which Mary Braddon knew from first-hand experience. When young James goes backstage, he had had a "vague idea that a green-room was a dazzling saloon, lighted by crystal chandeliers, lined with mirrors, and furnished with divans of ruby velvet"; instead he is shocked to find himself "in a small dingy chamber, carpetless, curtainless, uncleanly, provided with narrow baize-covered benches" (Ch. 2). He remarks that "seen from the outside there seems a not unpleasant Bohemian flavour about it—but when one comes behind the scenes the Bohemian flavour appears to be mainly dirt" (Ch. 2). The young heroine, Justina, is another victim of a selfish father. The pompous actor is not so much cruel to his daughter as simply unaware of her existence except as it contributes to his convenience.

The other heroine—they often come in pairs in Braddon's novels—is one of her most attractive characters. Madge Bellingham is not only beautiful and intelligent, she has moral strengths beyond those of the average young woman reared in the world of London society. She marries Churchill Penwyn out of deep love for him, unaware of the murder he had committed, partly for his own ambition, but even more in order that he might secure Madge for his wife. The ultimate revelation of his crime is moving in its tragedy for this admirable woman.

Madge Bellingham would have married Churchill without the money. The contrast between her values and the conventional views of "society" are wittily satirized in the character of Lady Cheshunt, who is delighted when Madge's suitor acquires a fortune, as she tells Madge: "Well, my dear, Providence has been very good to you; for, no doubt, if Mr. Penwyn had remained poor you'd have made a fool of yourself sooner or later for his sake, and gone to live in Bloomsbury, where even I couldn't have visited you, on account of my servants. One might get over that sort of thing one's self, but coachmen are so particular where they wait" (Ch. 15).

While professional detectives are usually treated in a favorable light by Mary Braddon, in *A Strange Story* two bumblers appear who recall Blathers and Duff in *Oliver Twist*. In their brief appearance, Higlett and Smelt, bearing tag names—not a usual device in Braddon's fiction—clumsily arrest an innocent man for the murder of James Penwyn. This early Dickensian lapse is uncommon, for she more often follows the attitude of admiration for the detective police which Dickens developed after 1850. As she said of the detective Henry Carter in *Henry Dunbar*, he was to be admired for doing a sometimes unpleasant task, necessary for the preservation of society:

> If he was called upon to worm out chance clues to guilty secrets in the careless confidence that grows out of a friendly glass; if at times he had to stoop to acts which, in other men, would be branded as shameful and treacherous, he knew that he did his duty, and that society could not hold together unless some such men as himself—clear-headed, brave, resolute, and unscrupulous in the performance of unpleasant work—were willing to act as watch-dogs for the protection of the general fold. (Ch. 38)

Of the minor writers of mystery fiction in the three decades before the advent of Conan Doyle, Mary Braddon is probably the finest craftsman. There is, of course, some padding inevitable in the production of such an incredible number of three-deckers; there is, at times, more sentimentality than modern taste would allow; in short, her work shares in the shortcomings of all but the greatest fiction of its period; but it also provides to-day's mystery fans with some delightful and rewarding reading.

JAMES PAYN

The popular "sensation" novelist, James Payn, was born at Cheltenham on February 28, 1830. In *Some Literary Recollections*, published in 1884, Payn describes his early years. His father, a country gentleman, tried to interest him in riding and hunting, but James preferred reading books and the companionship of his affectionate mother.[10] Like other sensitive boys who were not good at sports, he was miserable at prep school and at Eton, which he entered at the age of eleven. Even worse was the time spent at the school in Woolwich which prepared him for entrance to the Royal Military Academy. He detested the rigor and tedium of the studies, which left no time for reading and writing on his own. At last ill health secured his release, and he was sent to a tutor in Devonshire, where a charming teacher and pleasant surroundings for the first time made learning tolerable. Best of all were the ensuing years at Trinity College, Cambridge, where he thoroughly enjoyed university life, achieving some small recognition as the author of a volume of poems.

Payn's first prose publication, an article exposing conditions at the Woolwich Academy, was accepted by *Household Words*, at that time edited by Dickens, who was the young author's idol. After Cambridge, Payn continued contributing to magazines, and in 1858 went to live in Edinburgh where he became editor of *Chambers's Journal*. Meanwhile, he had married his fiancée, Louisa Edlin, whom he describes as "the source and cause of the happiness of my life."[11] A few years of the Scottish cold was enough for the family, and in 1861 they moved to London, where Payn continued to edit the *Journal* for another decade. Payn loved London, where he became a friend of Dickens and his circle and eventually knew everyone in the literary world.

His first major success came in 1864 with the publication of *Lost Sir Massingberd*, the popularity of which he calls "an epoch in my literary life."[12] From this time on, Payn's fiction paid well, his income eventually attaining the "four figures" that marked the achievement of the popular novelist. In 1874 he became a reader for the publishing firm of Smith, Elder, and from 1883 to 1896 edited their *Cornhill Magazine*. For a number of years he wrote a popular weekly column of lively anecdote in the *Illustrated London News*. In the *Dictionary of National Biography*, Leslie Stephen describes him as a man of great personal charm. "In his writing, as in his life, he was the simplest and least affected of men. He made no pretence [sic] to profound views of human nature, but overflowed with spontaneous vivacity and love of harmless fun." In his last years, Payn suffered uncomplainingly from painful rheumatism but continued to write. At his death in 1898 he was mourned by his wife and children and by a large circle of friends.

As editor of *Cornhill Magazine*, Payn was one of the first to accept the work of an unknown writer named Arthur Conan Doyle. When he published Doyle's story, "Habakuk Jephson's Statement" in 1884, it was a tribute to Doyle's promise, for the *Cornhill* was a distinguished journal known for seeking work of literary merit. It is true that in 1866 Payn declined *A Study in Scarlet*, which Doyle had submitted to him in hope it could be given serial publication before it came out in book form. In their *Catalogue of Crime*, Jacques Barzun and Wendell Hertig Taylor have described Payn's refusal as greatly to his "discredit,"[13] implying that Payn failed to recognize Doyle's abilities, but the facts are quite different. Payn wrote to Doyle, "I have kept your story an unconscionably long time, but it so interested me that I wanted to finish it. It's capital. [But] it's too long—and too short—for the 'Cornhill Magazine.'"[14] The problem of length was a crucial one. Too long for a single issue of the magazine, but too short to run as a serial, this first appearance of Sherlock Holmes in fiction was refused by Payn with great reluctance and with high praise for its merits. Later on, Payn accepted Doyle's *The White Company* for the *Cornhill*, even though he was "chary of historical novels,"[15] and warmly recommended Doyle to a representative of the American publisher Lippincott, for whom Doyle then wrote *The Sign of Four*.[16] Thus Payn admired and supported Doyle's work and was no doubt the first editor to read a Sherlock Holmes story, but ironically the popularity of Sherlock Holmes, coming near the end of Payn's own life, had little or no influence on his own fiction.

Like his fellow "sensation" novelists, James Payn did not confine himself to stories of crime or mystery in the more than forty novels he produced. Some are simply love stories or conventional tales of adventure, without elements of mystery. However, unlike Wilkie Collins and others, Payn did not turn to themes of social purpose, except for occasional observations on contemporary life. As Leslie Stephen wrote, "To Payn, it may be said, novel-writing meant simply straightforward story-telling; he had no wish to propound religious or social or psychological theories, or to embody a philosophical conception of human life. He never, like his master Dickens, wrote attacks upon political abuses, or aimed at emphasizing a particular moral."[17] The quality of Payn's novels is uneven. At his best, his fiction is entertaining, while at the other end of the spectrum it may be tedious and even absurd. A brief sampling of his novels will indicate his contribution to mystery fiction between 1860 and the end of the century.

When Payn's *Lost Sir Massingberd: A Romance of Real Life* appeared in 1864, its popularity no doubt owed much to the eagerness of the public for novels of mystery in the vein of *The Woman in White*, published four years earlier. That Payn was bidding for this market is clear. In his "Recollections" some twenty years later, he expressed his delight that Wilkie Collins, one of his "masters in the art of fiction," had told Payn that "he could not guess what had become of my missing baronet . . . till he came on the page that told him."[18]

Lost Sir Massingberd develops slowly, unlike Mary Braddon's *Lady Audley's Secret*, which for all its immaturity kept the reader agog with a rapid series of events. In the beginning, the narrator adopts the persona of an old-fashioned gentleman who declares that he will not tell his story in the "snappy, jerky" modern way, but in his own leisurely fashion, and he does so. Sir Massingberd, a classically

wicked baronet, lives on his neglected family estate where
he keeps gamekeepers and guard dogs to threaten the lives
of poachers and trespassers. The estate is entailed to the
baronet's nephew Marmaduke, whose life is under constant threat from his uncle. In a variation of the usual
Gothic pattern, it is the nephew rather than a young
woman who is in danger. The legalities of the plot are a
bit hazy, for the enormous income from the estate accrues
to the nephew and cannot be used by Sir Massingberd,
who has long since run through his own money. Nor-
mally, the uncle's life interest in the estate would give him
the income as well, but for purposes of the plot, he must
have a strong motive for disposing of his nephew before
the boy can marry and produce an heir. As the boy's sole
guardian, and the absolute monarch of his isolated manor,
one would expect that he would have eliminated this ob-
stacle to fortune long since, but somehow Marmaduke
survives to young manhood. The actual mystery in *Lost
Sir Massingberd* does not begin until beyond the halfway
point in the novel, when the baronet is reported missing,
and has presumably been murdered. From that point on,
the suspense is well handled, with a number of suspects
all provided with motives for doing away with the missing
man, including the butler, the gamekeeper, a band of
gypsies, and a mad wife. The final solution—which even
Wilkie Collins could not guess—is truly horrifying and
undoubtedly contributed to the notoriety of the novel.

An interesting feature of *Lost Sir Massingberd* is Payn's
introduction of Townshend, the famous Bow Street Runner. The story is set in the early 1820s—Sir Massingberd had

played whist for high stakes with George IV when he was Prince Regent—when the Runner Townshend was at the height of his career and was known to perform services for the monarch himself. Townshend is described in the novel in much the same glowing terms Dickens had used for Inspector Field and his fellow officers of the Detective Police. In fact, Payn refers to Townshend as "the father of all the Fields . . . of the present day" (Ch. 26). The renowned Bow Street officer, who was brought in to help solve the disappearance of Sir Massingberd, is described as a "short squab [sic] man, in a light wig, kerseymere breeches and a blue Quakercut coat . . . not, to look at, a very formidable object. But he possessed the courage of a lion, and the cunning of a fox. The ruffians who kept society in terror, themselves quailed before *him*. They knew that he was hard to kill, and valued not his own life one rush, when duty called upon him to hazard it" (Ch. 26). Townshend demonstrates his efficiency by tracing a series of bank notes by their serial numbers and by cynically exposing a con man who claims to have seen the missing baronet. In the end, Townshend successfully clears all the suspects connected with the bank notes but does not solve the mystery of the baronet's disappearance. Before the final disclosure, the narrator challenges the reader by declaring that anyone who can guess the secret is wiser than "the genius of Bow Street" (Ch. 30). The mystery, which is solved not by detection but by accident, sustains the reader's suspense until the last dramatic revelation.

Two years after *Sir Massingberd*, Payn made a much

less successful excursion into the realm of the Gothic novel. *The Clyffards of Clyffe* (1866) contains such a plethora of sensational devices and such stilted dialogue that a reader today is tempted to suspect it of parody until the length and seriousness of the novel discounts such a theory. There is a moated castle with priests' holes and secret passages; there is a beautiful blonde who, like Lady Audley, marries a much older man, but whose evil machinations make her prototype look like an angel; there is a family curse and inherited madness among the Clyffards; and there are not one but two sets of caves in which lives are threatened or taken. All of this is couched in narrative of high-flown sentiment and in incredible dialogue such as the following:

> *"She may make him jealous, Raymond."*
>
> *"Jealous!" echoed the young man, turning pale as the white column beside him—"jealous, of what? of whom? Not, Heaven forfend, of thee, Mildred?"*
>
> *"I say not of what, dear Ray," answered she hastily; "only beware! I know not what vile plots may be going on against us."*

Happily, Payn does not sink to this level of artificiality in most of his fiction. While the dialogue in other novels is often unduly formal, the characters inhabit a world much closer to reality than that of the Clyffards of Clyffe.

Like Father, Like Son (1871) is a more typical Payn crime novel. The father of the title is a wicked squire like Sir Massingberd, with differences of detail. Equally tyrannical, he still has money but is squandering it at a rate that will soon reduce him to poverty, or so his hangers-on fear. The squire refuses to acknowledge the legitimacy of his son Richard because of a technicality in the marriage. Again Payn's law is dubious: because the wife signed the license as "spinster" instead of "widow"—for she had been married before—the marriage was declared invalid although she was seven months pregnant when the squire decided to dispense with her. Since English common law tended to support the legitimacy of unborn children, and since she was married to the squire when the child was conceived, it is likely that she could have successfully contested the decision. In any case, the boy is called Richard Yorke and grows up bitterly hating the squire and vowing revenge.

Meanwhile, Richard goes to Cornwall to investigate a tin mine which is part of his father's estate, and which a rumor has indicated might have value. While there, he falls in love with the pretty daughter of an innkeeper and becomes embroiled in "borrowing" a large sum of money from the father's strongbox, which he intends to return. Detected with the money before he can return it, he is convicted of theft and sentenced to twenty years in prison. An interesting commentary on the changing society of the period occurs in the harshness of the sentence, which was attributed in part to the revelation that Richard had participated in a "new crime" for which there was as yet no prohibition. During the 1840s, the time at which these events took place, the British government had begun to offer competitive examinations for many appointments that had formerly been in the gift of politicians. Because

Richard was endowed with quick natural intelligence and a good education, he had accepted a fee from several young men to "sit" for them and pass the examinations, which they would no doubt have failed. Although Richard could apparently not be prosecuted for this offense, the judge regarded it as showing criminal tendency and lengthened his sentence accordingly.

After some grim and horrendous pictures of prison life and a sensational escape, the last portion of the novel presents some dramatic scenes in the abandoned mine and ties up other threads of its complex plot. While there are some commendable moments in *Like Father, Like Son*, the total effect is marred by the absence of any characters pleasant enough or strong enough to secure the reader's sympathy. Except for the innocent girl, the persons in the novel are uniformly greedy, conniving, or consumed with bitterness, with few redeeming features to flesh out their personalities. *Like Father, Like Son* represents what might be called the standard "sensation" novel of the period, in which the chief appeal to the reader lies in grisly details and scenes of horror.

Much better is *By Proxy* (1878), which outsold even *Sir Massingberd* to become Payn's most popular novel. The plot begins with the ingenious device of a man sacrificing his life for a friend in order to provide a fortune for his family, after which the friend fails to fulfill his part of the bargain. Captain Arthur Conway has accompanied his wealthy friend Ralph Pennicuick on an excursion into a remote area of China. Conway treats the native peoples and customs with courtesy and respect, while the arrogant

Pennicuick is boorish and contemptuous. Visiting a Buddhist shrine where the priest shows him a sacred gem called the Shay-Le, Pennicuick impulsively seizes an opportunity to take the diamond from its ancient pogoda. When he is arrested and sentenced to death by the Mandarin magistrates, Conway learns that he may offer himself as a "proxy" at the execution and strikes the bargain with the now terrified Pennicuick that the sum of twenty thousand pounds will be paid to Conway's wife and daughter after his death. Amid scenes of Chinese torture which are not for the squeamish, Pennicuick leaves his friend to his fate, returns to England, and then realizes that, with no evidence of their pact, he can simply refrain from paying over the money.

The son and daughter of the two men have grown up together and are now in love, but Nelly Conway, in true Victorian fashion, refuses to marry Raymond Pennicuick because she is poor and he is rich. Hence the villainy of the elder Pennicuick is not merely base and cowardly but obstructs the course of romance.

When Ralph Pennicuick decides to run for a seat in Parliament, Payn gives his readers a gently satirical picture of the electoral process. With no political experience nor even any convictions, the candidate with a generous purse and the proper sponsorship can compete, although with no guarantee of success. In the Midland county for which he has been put up, Pennicuick duly goes about addressing the farmers and small tradespeople of the area, accompanied by his local sponsor. Having always had "a high idea of the stupidity of his fellow-creatures" (Ch. 37), Pennicuick finds his opinion confirmed by the attention of his audience, without realizing that in rural areas any kind of free entertainment will draw a crowd. The same arrogance that he displayed toward the Chinese prevails in his attitude toward his fellow countrymen in any class below his own. This man, who "had never so much as spoken to a greengrocer . . . in all of his life," feels that the canvassing process is somehow degrading. "He had a positive feeling of humiliation in saying that same thing over and over again, in district A, in district B, and district C, and especially, as sometimes happened, to the same people." Ironically, when the election results are in, Pennicuick is the winner, but he has already "begun to think that Parliamentary life would bore him a good deal, and interest him scarcely at all" (Ch. 37).

The theme of the sacred gem from a Far Eastern shrine, used so memorably by Wilkie Collins in *The Moonstone* a decade earlier, was a sure-fire device for catching the imagination of Payn's readers. In *By Proxy* the pattern of *The Moonstone* is reversed: we know who took the stone but the suspense lies in how Pennicuick's betrayal of his friend will be revealed. Although the Shay-Le had been returned to the temple, there was still a curse upon the man who had desecrated the shrine, and he must not go unpunished. Despite some lengthy passages of sentimental "filler," the ending of the novel is well devised. Nevertheless, while *By Proxy* is one of Payn's better novels, it does not approach the merit of Wilkie Collins's best work.

Jewels figure again in one of Payn's best crime novels, *A Confidential Agent* (1880). An extremely valuable diamond necklace belonging to Lady Pargiter disappears, along with the "confidential agent" who regularly delivers it to her when she wishes to wear it and then returns it to the safe of the jeweler's firm where he is employed. With Payn's typical leisurely opening, it is not until the end of the first of three volumes that the disappearance occurs, but once the action begins, it moves briskly and becomes admirably suspenseful. Despite its moderate pace, the opening volume lays the foundation for the ensuing mystery by introducing a group of attractive characters in a tranquil domestic setting which enhances the horror that follows. The jeweler's agent, Matthew Helston, is an intelligent and sensitive young man with a bent for mechanical invention, utterly devoted to his wife Sabey, in whose character Payn manages to make simple goodness attractive. Genteel people of limited means, they live with Matthew's Uncle Stephen, a kindly eccentric, and Sabey's sister, Amy, a charming and independent young woman.

When Matthew and the diamond necklace first disappear, various theories of the crime begin to circulate. Many people assume that Matthew has been murdered by thieves who made off with the diamonds, but when no dead body is found, suspicion falls on Matthew in spite of his impeccable reputation for honesty. Also suspected is Rutherford, the Dickensian cab driver who always drove for Matthew on the occasions when he carried the diamonds. Whether Rutherford acted in collusion with Matthew or was in league with a set of thieves who attacked Matthew, in either case he is strongly believed to be implicated in the crime.

Another theory is that held by Mr. Signet, the jeweler, who firmly believes that Lady Pargiter has kept the diamonds herself in order to claim compensation from him and that she has had Matthew detained or even murdered in order to sustain the fiction of the theft.

Presently, circumstantial evidence begins to appear that points to Matthew's guilt. He is reported to have been seen in Paris, in company with an attractive young woman, attempting to sell some unset diamonds to a jeweler there. That the young woman was the first love of his youth, who had left him to go off with another man, makes the evidence all the more damaging. Only Sabey and Amy never lose faith in his innocence. Amy's fiancé, a young solicitor named Frank Barlow, initially takes the role of the detective, following up a series of clues which seem to confirm the evidence against Matthew. The careful establishment of Matthew's honesty in the opening scenes of the novel now underscores the suspense for the reader. Just as in Collins's *The Moonstone* the established truthfulness of Rachel Verinder appeared to confirm the impossible, so in *A Confidential Agent* it is incongruous to think of the gentle and serious Matthew as being involved in theft and adultery. In the end, the fact that the actual culprit bore an outward resemblance to Matthew is presented convincingly, with less than the usual contrivance, to account for the mistaken identity. The final honors go to the Scotland Yard detective who discovers the vacant house where Matthew has in fact been held prisoner since the night the diamonds were taken.

When Payn introduced into *A Confidential Agent* the suspicion that Lady Pargiter had kept her own diamonds in order to collect their value from the jeweler, he has playing upon a theme familiar to his contemporary readers from Anthony Trollope's novel *The Eustace Diamonds* (1873), which had appeared some seven years earlier. In this third of Trollope's six novels in the "Palliser" series, the beautiful young widow Lizzie Eustace refuses to give up the enormously valuable diamond necklace, which she claims as her own although it is regarded by the Eustace family as an heirloom. She carries it about with her in a specially made iron box, refusing to deposit it with jewelers in the fear that the Eustace family lawyer will seize it. The necklace is "stolen" twice in the course of the novel. On the first occasion the iron box is taken from Lizzie's hotel room in Carlisle while the diamonds, unknown to the thieves, are safely tucked away under the sleeping Lizzie's pillow. When she learns of the theft, she cannot resist the temptation to let the world believe them to be stolen, thus escaping the threats of legal action for their return. On the second occasion, when the diamonds are in fact stolen, she now cannot claim them as missing. Trollope, who always affected to despise elements of plot construction in novels, implies his rejection of the mystery formula by telling the reader in the first instance that Lizzie still has the diamonds: "He who recounts these details," says the narrator piously, "has scorned to have a secret between himself and his readers." Nevertheless, when the diamonds are actually taken, he does not tell the reader at once who has taken them, maintaining a little mystery sequence despite his tongue-in-cheek disclaimer.

With the example of Trollope's Lizzie Eustace before them, Payn's readers of *A Confidential Agent* were no doubt inclined to believe that Lady Pargiter was, like Lizzie Eustace, in some way guilty of arranging the theft of her own diamond necklace, so that Payn gained a twist in suspense by undercutting their expectation. While the plot device of disappearing diamonds was a popular one, both Trollope and Payn lend significance to the incidents through moral and social commentary. In *The Eustace Diamonds* the jewels themselves become a symbol of Lizzie's selfishness and greed, fostered by a society which encourages marriages contracted for monetary gain and which despises the simple virtues. Similarly, in *A Confidential Agent* Payn condemns the artifices of Lady Pargiter and the society in which she moves. Matthew Helston, who loathed being patronized by this worthless woman, felt degraded by having to serve her. In his view, "the crowds who thronged Lady Pargiter's house in Moor Street on her rout nights, and paid court to her, and admired her diamonds, were themselves not in a wholesome state of mind. What was there in such a woman to attract anyone? What worth, apart from money's worth, did she possess? What intelligence? what virtue? what merit? Why, in the name of Heaven (or even of common sense), because she was a money-lender's daughter, and had succeeded to his ill-got Ingot gains, should she be proud?"

Of James Payn's total output in fiction, the works of crime and suspense are outnumbered by his domestic novels and tales of adventure. However, while Payn is not in the first rank of Victorian writers, some of his best "sensation" novels make a worthwhile contribution to the newly emerging mystery form.

ANNA KATHARINE GREEN

The first thing that strikes the reader of Anna Katharine Green's novels is that they sound like modern mystery stories. Their central purpose is to use a crime as a direct puzzle for the reader to solve and they waste no time in getting on with the plot. Wilkie Collins, as has been shown, developed the mystery formula almost by accident, while intent upon writing novels of character and incident. Le Fanu wavered between social comedy and Gothic horror in much of his work. Mary Braddon and James Payn often used sensational crime plots in the manner of Collins, but both engaged in lengthy digressions in order to satisfy serial publication and to fill up the three volumes required by the circulating libraries. As an American, Anna Green was free to publish her novels directly in one-volume book form, and their comparative brevity and refreshing directness helped to keep the focus on the tightly constructed plots. Her chief models were the detective stories of Edgar Allan Poe and the Monsieur Lecoq tales of Emile Gaboriau.[19] Published in 1878, her first mystery novel, *The Leavenworth Case*, came out nine years before Conan Doyle's Sherlock Holmes made his first appearance and anticipated with remarkable originality many of the characteristics of subsequent mystery fiction.

Born in New York city in 1846, the youngest daughter of a prominent lawyer, Anna Katharine Green lived in the affluent society immortalized by her famous contemporary Edith Wharton. Anna attended Ripley Female College in Poultney, Vermont, and later received a B.A. degree from Green Mountain Junior College (where incidentally she had initiated Ralph Waldo Emerson into a secret society.)[20] For a number of years she wrote poetry without much recognition, finally turning to the writing of mystery fiction, where she met with immediate success, *The Leavenworth Case* alone eventually selling more than 750,000 copies.[21] In 1884 she married Charles Rohlfs, who had been an actor for some years. They settled in Buffalo, where Rohlfs managed a foundry and later became a funiture designer. The couple had three children and were active in community affairs. For more than forty years, Anna Green's mystery fiction continued to sell; her last novel, *The Step on the Stair*, came out in 1923, twelve years before her death in 1935.

A notable feature of Anna Katharine Green's work is that she was able to turn out one ingenious plot after another in more than thirty novels and several volumes of short stories. Of course, some are better than others, but her relative consistency is impressive. Despite her immense popularity, her work fell quickly into obscurity after 1920, no doubt because she remained a Victorian to the last. When the first World War wrought dramatic social change and brought in its wake, on both sides of the Atlantic, the rejection of Victorian and Edwardian codes of behavior, Anna Green was already in her seventies. Her characters had always remained in what was now regarded as the quaintly tiresome society in which men and women talked seriously about Honor and Duty, or made noble self-sacrifices in the cause of Love. Nevertheless, within such limitations, her characters are often charmingly developed and are far from cardboard figures.

Green's first novel, *The Leavenworth Case: A Lawyer's Story* (1878) begins with characteristic briskness. By the end of the first brief chapter, Everett Raymond, the lawyer of the subtitle, has been summoned to the house where the elderly philanthropist, Mr. Leavenworth, has been shot. Raymond is greeted at the door by the detective, Ebenezer Gryce; the coroner's inquest is ready to begin; he is shown the body; and the reader is provided with a diagram of the library and adjoining bedroom which constitute the scene of the crime. There had been no robbery; the doors of the house were locked; in short, as Trueman Harwell, the secretary to Mr. Leavenworth, declares, "The whole affair is a mystery." This could be the opening of an Agatha Christie novel, some forty years before *The Mysterious Affair at Styles* introduced Hercule Poirot to the world in 1921. Already, Green is using in this novel a number of devices which become familiar in classic detective fiction of the twentieth century. At the inquest, an expert witness identifies the bullet as coming from the murder weapon; later on, the detective, Mr. Gryce, remarks that yellow paper burns differently from white, and traces paper according to the quire from which it came. Even the use of illustrations is modern: in addition to more than one floor plan, there are reproductions of the strips of a letter from which a message is reconstructed, a device later used by Conan Doyle in "The Reigate Squires." Most important, perhaps, is the emphasis upon the medical evidence indicating the position of the victim's head and the distance from which the shot was fired, as well as the approximate time of death.

Green's use of the young lawyer Everett Raymond as the narrator of the story provides an excellent means of sustaining suspense. The characters are seen as he perceives them, from the colorless secretary to the breathtakingly beautiful Leavenworth girls, the nieces of the murdered man. Although Mary's beauty is more dazzling, Raymond is clearly enamored of Eleanore at first sight, giving rise to some ingenious ambiguities as suspicion falls upon each of the characters in turn in a brilliant whodunit pattern. Raymond also becomes a forerunner of Dr. Watson as he admiringly describes Gryce's methods of detection, thus glorifying the figure of the detective.

Although Anna Green struck out in a new direction from her English contemporaries in the tight construction of her mystery plots, her celebrated detective is very much in the tradition of Inspector Bucket and Sergeant Cuff and as unlike Poe's Auguste Dupin as were the detectives of Dickens and Collins. A member of the New York police, Mr. Gryce is even more modest than his prototypes. When he asks Raymond at one point to assist him, it is because Raymond is a "gentleman" who can move with ease in the world of wealth and social distinction of the Leavenworths. Less brash than Inspector Bucket, who did not hesitate to speak his mind to Sir Leicester Dedlock, Gryce nevertheless maintains his own dignity when the occasion requires. Described as "a portly, comfortable personage," Gryce has the endearing eccentricity of rarely looking directly at the person with him. If his eye "rested anywhere, it was always on some insignificant object in the vicinity, some vase, inkstand, book, or button. These things he would seem to take into his confidence, make the repositories of his conclusions" (Ch. 1). When Raymond remarks that the situation looks dreadful, "Mr. Gryce immediately frowned at the door-knob," but his eyes never miss anything of importance, as Raymond soon learns: "Mr. Gryce was seemingly observant of my glance, though his own was fixed upon the chandelier" (Ch. 1). In moments of stress, he consults a fly on Raymond's sleeve or holds "a close and confidential confab with his finger-tips."

Despite his deceptively casual manner, however, Gryce can become electrified when a series of discoveries seems to lead to a solution of the mystery. He will not give up until he has learned the full truth. "It is a principle which every detective recognizes," he declares, "that if of a hundred leading circumstances connected with a crime, ninety-nine of these are acts pointing to the suspected party with unerring certainty, but the hundredth equally important act is one which that person could not have performed, the whole fabric of suspicion is destroyed" (Ch. 37). Sherlock Holmes could not have said more.

Mr. Gryce reappears off and on throughout the course of Green's fiction. Following the pattern introduced by Poe when he used the character of Auguste Dupin in three stories, Green gives the detecting honors to Mr. Gryce in a dozen or so of her novels. Writers of the English school had not as yet used the technique of carrying a detective through a series of stories, probably because the detective was still not the central focus of interest. Today's readers regret, for example, that Sergeant Cuff appears only in *The Moonstone* and that Wilkie Collins did not use him again in subsequent tales of detection. In France, the pattern had been used by Gaboriau in his series of crime stories featuring the detective exploits of Monsieur Lecoq and Père Tabaret. In England, it was Conan Doyle who set the pattern for future generations when he conceived the plan of doing a series of Sherlock Holmes stories for the *Strand Magazine* in 1891, bringing immense popularity to his Great Detective. Anna Green thus anticipated Doyle by several years in the device of the reappearing detective.

One of Anna Green's finest novels is *Hand and Ring* (1883), with its excellent characters and its brilliantly developed mystery plot. The story opens with a group of gentlemen conversing about crime while standing on the courthouse steps in the New York town of Sibley. A stranger in the group, later identified as Mr. Gryce, suggests that the most successful crime is one committed in a place open to view and with many passersby, pointing out a plain little house opposite as an example. A few minutes later, the widow who occupies the house is found dead, and so the plot begins to spin. A number of suspects are provided with motive and opportunity. Imogene Dare—another heroine of dazzling beauty—and her lover each suspect the other of the crime. This device, seeming at first to be fortuitous, becomes startlingly convincing as clue after clue appears indicating that each has good reason for suspicion of the other. There is a coroner's inquest, always well-handled in Green's works, and later on a fine courtroom scene.

The detecting in *Hand and Ring* is done initially by young Mr. Byrd, a "gentleman" detective from New York, aided by a less scrupulous assistant named Hickory. Both are competent enough up to a point, but in the end Mr. Gryce arrives to make the final deductions and wrap up the case. Since *Hand and Ring* was Green's fifth novel and marks the third appearance of Mr. Gryce, her readers were no doubt by this time prepared to recognize him by his eccentricities even before he was named. Thus the heroine, hearing a "bland and fatherly voice over her shoulder," turns and sees a strange gentleman:

> She saw before her a large comfortable-looking personage of middle age, of no great pretensions to elegance or culture, but bearing that within his face which oddly enough baffled her understanding while it encouraged her trust. This was the more peculiar in that he was not looking at her, but stood with his eyes fixed on the fading light of the hall-lamp, which he surveyed with an expression of concern that almost amounted to pity. (Ch. 38)

Just as Agatha Christie's readers would recognize as Hercule Poirot a dapper little man in pointed shoes who twirled his mustache and spoke of his "little gray cells," Green's readers would know that Mr. Gryce had arrived when the fatherly person bent his gaze of pity not upon Imogene but upon the hall-lamp.

In addition to the lovable Mr. Gryce, Anna Green

created another detective figure in the person of Amelia Butterworth, a middle-aged spinster from one of the old families of New York. In *That Affair Next Door* (1897) Miss Butterworth, from her strategically placed window, sees mysterious comings and goings in the Van Burnam mansion next door to her own. When the dead body of a young woman is discovered in the presumably de-serted house and Mr. Gryce is sent to investigate, Miss Butterworth discovers her own undeveloped talents for detection. At first Mr. Gryce does not take her seri-ously, beyond recognizing her superior knowledge in matters of hatpins, bonnets, pincushions, and petti-coats, but he soon comes to respect her keen mind and practical good sense. The sparring between them is han-dled with the deftness of high comedy, as Amelia, who narrates the novel, describes her own persistence in tracking down clues despite Mr. Gryce's gentle hints that she withdraw into ladylike seclusion. In the end, Gryce, with characteristic modesty, admits that he has been mistaken and that Amelia was on the right track. When she tells him of her crucial discoveries, he ex-presses his delight. "You have saved me from commit-ting a folly, Miss Butterworth," he tells her. "If I had arrested Franklin Van Burnam today, and to-morrow all these facts had come to light, I should never have held up my head again."

Anticipating such famous spinster sleuths as Agatha Cristie's Miss Marple and Dorothy Sayers's Miss Climp-son, who sometimes assists Lord Peter Wimsey, Amelia Butterworth appears in several other novels, always in conjunction with the inimitable Mr. Gryce. The best of these, in addition to the excellent *That Affair Next Door*, are *Lost Man's Lane* (1898), and *The Circular Study* (1900). In the latter story, incidentally, Green shows a fondness for gadgetry worthy of James Bond, depicting the study as a circular room containing colored electric light signals and a steel door which closes at the touch of a button and cannot be reopened.

Not content with one female detective, Anna Green introduced another in the character of Violet Strange, in *The Golden Slipper* (1915). A young and charming debutante, Violet uses her access to the inner circle of wealthy New York society to solve a series of problems for which she is highly paid by a private agency. Each case is a challenge to Violet's analytical powers and a thread of mystery runs through the series as the reader wonders why this young girl with a wealthy and indulgent father is so desperate for money that she reluctantly and secretly takes the assignments of her employers. In the end, her goal is revealed. Aided by her brother, and ultimately by the man whom she freed from suspicion of murder and whom she eventually marries, Violet has accumulated enough money to rescue a beloved sister who had been disinherited. Despite some improbabilities and some touches of Gothic horror, including a secret passage to a sealed room where dead bodies are interred, the Violet Strange stories are pleasantly entertaining and contain many of the felicitous character studies which adorn Anna Green's work. Moreover, in both of her lady detectives, Green is clearly underscoring the intellectual capabilities of women in an age which was all too ready to relegate the fair sex to the drawing room and the nursery. Amelia Butterworth and Violet Strange are capable, forthright, enterprising women without simper or sentimentality, and while Green is never polemical, the accomplishments of her lady detectives speak for themselves.

Anna Green's influence on writers of mystery fiction may be more extensive than we know. Her work was widely read on both sides of the Atlantic and may well have had its effect upon the "genteel" school of detective fiction which developed rapidly in Great Britain in the early years of the twentieth century. Certainly she must have been the model for writers of the American school such as Mary Roberts Rinehart, whose work resembles that of her predecessor. Green's originality, the tightness of her plots, the attractiveness of her characters, and her astonishing consistency over a forty-five year span make her an author well worth a second look, while the old-fashioned qualities which banished her to obscurity have now, in an age of Victorian revival, taken on a patina of charm.

6

Arthur Conan Doyle and the Great Detective

In a series such as *Recognitions*, of which this book is a part, the creator of Sherlock Holmes, like Charles Dickens, needs no recognition in the same sense as those lesser-known writers who have been treated in this volume. It is nevertheless fitting that an account of Victorian masters of mystery should conclude with a look at the crowning achievement of Arthur Conan Doyle. The Holmes stories form the pivot between the nineteeth and twentieth centuries in the development of the mystery genre, representing the culmination of half a century of experiments and marking out a formula that, for the next hundred years, has been either followed or rejected but never ignored.

Arthur Conan Doyle was born in 1859 to an Irish family that had settled in Edinburgh. His father's father had been a well-known artist and caricaturist, and Doyle's father inherited his artistic talent but not his ambition. In his autobiography, *Memories and Adventures*, Doyle describes his father as a genteel but dreamy man whose salary as a Civil Servant was scarcely adequate to maintain the ever-increasing family.[1] It was his mother who earned Doyle's admiration and gratitude for her management of the affairs of the household and for her unfailing ambition for her children.

Like other boys from good Catholic families, Doyle attended Hodder and then Stonyhurst, the Catholic counterpart of the English Eton. Much as he disliked the tedious curriculum and the severity of the discipline, he survived better than most because of his large physique and his success in games. He enjoyed a year at a German school, and on his return was entered as a medical student at Edinburgh University, where one of his professors, Dr. Joseph Bell, later became the inspiration for Sherlock Holmes.

After tours of duty as ship's surgeon on an Arctic whaler and on a voyage to West Africa, Doyle began medical practice in Portsmouth, where the paucity of patients gave him plenty of time to write stories for magazines, supplementing his meager income with a few guineas from an occasional acceptance. The practice gradually increased, reaching by the third year an income of about three hundred pounds. In 1885 Doyle fell in love with Louise Hawkins, a gentle and affectionate woman much like Dr. Watson's Mary Morstan. After several years of marriage and two children, Louise developed tuberculosis, and the family went to live in Switzerland and elsewhere in pursuit of her health, returning to England for some years before her death in 1906. Meanwhile, Doyle had become so successful as a writer that he was able to give up medical practice. He had left Portsmouth for several months' study of the eye in Vienna, returning to London where he set up as an eye surgeon and never received a single patient. At this point, he joyfully abandoned medicine in order to follow the profession he loved.

During the Boer War, he went to South Africa as a doctor, observing at first hand the complexities of that conflict. On his return, he published a pamphlet entitled "The Cause and Conduct of the War in South Africa," which managed to be so objective in its analysis and yet so supportive of the British cause that it had an enormous circulation both at home and abroad and resulted in his knighthood. It was for this that he became Sir Arthur, and not for his creation of the already famous Sherlock Holmes, as mystery fans have sometimes supposed.

As early as his medical school days, Doyle had begun to feel that religious belief could not be reconciled with the new scientific thought of the Darwin and Huxley school. Like many another young Victorian intellectual, he found himself driven to agnosticism, while firmly stating that his position "never for an instant degenerated into atheism."[2] In his lifelong search for a substitute for his lost religion, Doyle early on became fascinated with spiritualist theory and eventually devoted his principal energies in his last years to writing and speaking in the promulgation of what became for him a creed.

After the First World War, he produced only occasional

fiction, while a new volume on spiritualism appeared almost every year. One of these, *The Coming of the Fairies* (1922), has only recently received worldwide publicity, as the two young Yorkshire girls, whose photographs of fairies taken in 1917 were accepted by Doyle as genuine, have at last confessed that the whole thing was a hoax.[3] Whether even this revelation would have shaken Doyle's faith is doubtful, for his belief was based upon a genuine need to find spiritual comfort in a material world. Accompanied by his beautiful and devoted second wife, whom he had married in 1907, Doyle traveled extensively in the service of the spiritualist cause until his death in 1930.

For nearly a century the character of Sherlock Holmes has so enchanted readers that he has become a cult figure; he is the subject of literally hundreds of articles and books, the source for the sale of countless deerstalker caps and other paraphernalia, and is commemorated by a pub in London where his sitting room at 221B Baker Street is reproduced in every detail, down to the Persian slipper and the coal scuttle. Such worship makes it all the more surprising that Holmes did not achieve immediate popularity when he first appeared. Doyle sent his manuscript of *A Study in Scarlet* to several publishers before it was accepted by Ward, Lock, and Co. for the grand sum of twenty-five pounds. James Payn had wanted it for the *Cornhill*, as mentioned in Chapter 5, but found its length awkward for the magazine. Ward & Co. solved this problem by bringing it out in *Beeton's Christmas Annual* for 1887, where its anomalous length could be accommodated.

To trace the origin of Sherlock Holmes, we must look

first at Doyle's earlier attempts at fiction. Like all fledgling authors, Doyle wanted to get his name before the public. Short stories were usually published anonymously; hence, he realized by 1886 that he "could go on doing short stories for ever and never make headway. What is necessary is that your name should be on the back of a volume."[4] His first attempt at the novel form was *The Firm of Girdlestone,* which he described in his memoirs as "a sensational book of adventure . . . too reminiscent of the work of others."[5]

By 1887, *Girdlestone* had made the usual round of publishers and been rejected. It is not an altogether bad novel; it is merely so conventional that it makes the freshness and originality of the Holmes work all the more remarkable. The plot, with strong echoes of Le Fanu's *Uncle Silas*, concerns the plight of the heroine whose father's will made her the ward of his friend, John Girdlestone, who will also inherit her fortune if she dies before coming of age. Financial reverses cause the miserly old man to try first to marry Kate to his evil son Ezra, and when she refuses, to imprison her in an isolated country house where she is to be murdered.

With its idealized scenes of romantic love, its long digressions into matters extraneous to the plot and its scenes of Gothic horror, *Girdlestone* is a typical product of the sensation school of fiction of the 1880s. While some writers on Doyle have seen *Girdlestone's* literary sources in Dickens[6] and Meredith,[7] no one seems to have noted that the novel most markedly resembles the fiction of James Payn, whose works Doyle admired and whom he regarded with "reverence" and "awe" at their first meeting.[8] The scenes of action and excitement in *Girdlestone*, like those in Payn's best work, are the most effective portions of the novel, while the "filler" scenes are often mediocre.

The description of the young hero in *Girdlestone* could be a portrait of Doyle himself. A medical student at Edinburgh University, young Tom Dimsdale is tall and broad in the chest, with a round, strong head on a muscular neck, and a face "Anglo-Saxon to the last feature, with its honest breadth between the eyes and its nascent moustache. . . . Shy, and yet strong; plain, and yet pleasing." Fond of boxing and a star performer at football, like his creator, Tom gives us a charming picture of the young Doyle. He does not, however, show any incipient talent for detection. When, later in the novel, he tries to follow Ezra Girdlestone in order to learn where poor Kate is incarcerated, his attempts are so inept that it is hard to believe that within a few short months after completing *Girdlestone*, Doyle was creating the inimitable Sherlock.

When the manuscript of *Girdlestone* was at last relegated to the back of a drawer, Doyle tells us that he now felt ready to try something "fresher and crisper":

> Gaboriau had rather attracted me by the neat dovetailing of his plots, and Poe's masterful detective, M. Dupin, had from boyhood been one of my heroes. But could I bring an addition of my own? I thought of my old teacher Joe Bell, of his eagle face, of his curious ways, of his eerie trick of spotting details. If he were a detective he would surely reduce this fascinating but unorganized business to

something nearer to an exact science. I would try if I could get this effect.[9]

While studying surgery with the famous Professor Bell, it had been Doyle's task to show the patients in, whereupon Bell, surrounded by students, would often make a series of deductions from a patient's appearance. He might say to a civilian that he had served in the army, was not long discharged, served in a Highland regiment, was a noncommissioned officer, and was stationed at Barbados, all of which seemed miraculous until it was clarified:

"You see, gentlemen," he would explain, "the man was a respectful man but did not remove his hat. They do not in the army, but he would have learned civilian ways had he been long discharged. He has an air of authority and he is obviously Scottish. As to Barbados, his complaint is elephantiasis, which is West Indian and not British."[10]

Here was the source for Holmes's great powers of observation, while the tight plots of the French school were combined with some of the characteristics of Poe's Dupin to produce the world's most famous fictional detective.

Sherlock Holmes represents a complete departure from the long tradition of the English detective—from the Bow Street Runners to the London Detective Police and their fictional counterparts. Unlike the Buckets and Cuffs, Holmes is a gentleman of good family, a university man, and an arrogant intellectual. Like Auguste Dupin, he regards the official police as plodding at best and inept at worst. Although he sometimes takes fees for his work, his attitude is entirely that of a dilettante. He takes only those cases that interest him and often works for no fee if the cause is just or the case sufficiently challenging. Fascinating as Holmes is in his own right, however, he would be incomplete without his faithful narrator, as Doyle at once realized: "He could not tell his own exploits," Doyle recounts, "so he must have a commonplace comrade as a foil—an educated man of action who could both join in the exploits and narrate them. A drab, quiet name for this unostentatious man. Watson would do. And so I had my puppets and wrote my 'Study in Scarlet.'"

In *A Study in Scarlet* (1887), their first appearance, Holmes and Watson exhibit in one way or another nearly all of the characteristics that have since become immortal. When they meet, Holmes exclaims, "You have been in Afghanistan, I perceive!" Holmes conducts his scientific experiments—he has just discovered a new test for bloodstains. They move into the rooms at 221B Baker Street, where clients come to Holmes, often from the police. He describes Gregson and Lestrade as "the pick of a bad lot of Scotland Yarders" (Ch. 3). Although Holmes's first injections of cocaine take place at the opening of the second novel, *The Sign of Four*, there is a hint in *A Study in Scarlet* of Watson's suspicion that Holmes's occasional "dreamy, vacant expression" might be due to the use of a narcotic (Ch. 2). The street urchins who become the Baker Street Irregulars make their first appearance in this novel. Holmes is already shown as being not absolutely infallible, for he laughs at himself at being taken in by the "old woman" who comes for the ring. And, of course, Holmes plays his violin. Since Doyle himself knew nothing of music, it might have been better had he endowed Holmes with another hobby, for although Watson testifies that his friend's technique is excellent, Holmes not only places the violin across his knees and "scrapes" upon it, but he also eagerly looks forward to a recital in which a noted violinist is billed to play Chopin!

Holmes's detective techniques in *A Study in Scarlet* set the pattern for that combination of armchair deduction and active pursuit of clues that characterizes all of his subsequent work. In addition to engaging in analytical reasoning, he studies the wheel marks of a hansom cab, examines elaborate patterns of footsteps, identifies cigar ash, and in the end engages in the detailed step-by-step summary of his methods that has become indispensable to the mystery format. Although Doyle wittily allows Holmes to tell Watson that Gaboriau's Lecoq was a "miserable bungler" and that Poe's Dupin "had some analytical genius, no doubt, but . . . was by no means such a phenomenon as Poe appeared to imagine" (Ch. 2), it is clear that his boyhood idol, Auguste Dupin, is the chief source for Holmes. Both are brilliant analysts, both are arrogant and impatient of lesser brains, and both are gentlemen of leisure who engage in detection primarily for its intellectual challenge.

While waiting for his *A Study in Scarlet* to appear in print, Doyle turned to writing his first historical novel,

Micah Clarke, set in the time of England's civil war between the Puritans and the Royalists. This was Doyle's
first attempt at what he regarded as his "serious" work,
and thus began the conflict in his own mind between the
Sherlock Holmes stories, which he felt were frivolous,
and his desire to become a distinguished man of letters
through his historical fiction—a modern day Sir Walter
Scott. When *Micah Clarke* appeared in 1889 to glowing
reviews, Doyle had every reason to believe that he had
found his metier.[17] He had already turned with enthusiasm to a study of the Middle Ages, attracted by the theme
of knightly honor. Now, with the success of *Micah*, he
threw himself heart and soul into the writing of a novel
set in the days of chivary.

In his excellent biography of Doyle, John Dickson Carr
suggests that the code of the knight was deeply ingrained
in Doyle's own nature. "When he went out into the great
world, and towered up against meanness or injustice, mil-
lions who never met him could hear the fervour of that
code just as they felt it in his books. It explains why the
book he loved best was the one he now prepared to
write—*The White Company*."[13] Thus, when the American
editor of *Lippincott's Magazine*, having read *A Study in Scarlet*, met with Doyle in London and asked him to do another Sherlock Holmes story, Doyle tossed off *The Sign of
Four*, regarding it lightly as a piece of busy-work. So en-
grossed was he in *The White Company* that at the time of
its composition he never mentioned *The Sign of Four* in letter, notebook, or diary.[14] No wonder, then, that Watson's wound in the shoulder from a Jezail bullet, which

had caused him such distress in *A Study in Scarlet*, has unaccountably shifted to his leg in *The Sign of Four*, where the wound from the same Jezail bullet causes him to limp painfully. Except for reading the proofs of *The Firm of Girdlestone*, which after the success of *Micah* had been retrieved from the back of the drawer and was now being published, Doyle concentrated all his attention upon his new novel. And his confidence was justified, for when he sent the completed manuscript to James Payn, who detested historical novels, Payn nevertheless accepted it at once for the *Cornhill* and called it the "best historical novel since *Ivanhoe*."[15]

It was during the very year in which *The White Company* was running in *Cornhill Magazine*—January to December 1891—that Sherlock Holmes leaped into fame. The two short Holmes novels had attracted little attention, and Doyle toyed with the idea of a series of short stories with a single character running through them, thus binding the reader to the magazine without the risk of missing an installment of a serial and hence losing interest in the story.[16] Doyle's newly acquired literary agent, the competent A. P. Watt, sent "A Scandal in Bohemia" to a new magazine called *The Strand*, and by December, when the sixth Holmes story appeared, the public—and *The Strand*—were wild for more. Doyle wrote to his mother that he would ask the absurd price of £50 for each story—he had received about £35 each for the first group—and was astonished when the magazine accepted. Already at the end of 1891 he wrote, to his mother's horror, that he was thinking of "slaying Holmes in the last and winding him up for good. He takes my mind from better things."[17] Absorbed already in a new historical novel, *The Refugees*, dealing with French Huguenots in Canada in the seventeenth century, Doyle regarded the Holmes stories as an unnecessary distraction.

When Doyle did send Holmes and Moriarty over the Reichenbach Falls to their presumed deaths, readers were stricken. The book sales of the first two collections—*The Adventures* and *The Memoirs*—were so lucrative that Doyle eventually gave way and brought out an "earlier" episode from Holmes's life in the splendid *The Hound of the Baskervilles* (1902). Finally he relented and brought him back to life in *The Return of Sherlock Holmes* (1905), then banished him into retirement on the Sussex Downs where he engaged in raising bees. Like an opera singer making a series of "farewell" performances, Holmes reappeared in *The Valley of Fear* (1915) and in *His Last Bow* (1917), which was not in fact the last, for the *Casebook* came out in 1927, three years before Doyle's death.

Doyle did not depend on the Holmes stories alone for financial success, popular as they were. Everything that came from his pen sold well. His historical and adventure fiction was widely read and loved, including the Brigadier Gerard stories and others. He wrote domestic novels and experimented with science fiction in the Professor Challenger stories, in addition to his extensive nonfiction. His reluctance to bring out Sherlock Holmes stories except under pressure stemmed from his resentment at the public clamor for work he regarded as undistinguished. In his memoirs, he sums up his grievance: "All things find their level, but I believe that if I had never touched Holmes, who has tended to obscure my higher work, my position in literature would at the present moment be a more commanding one."[18]

It is understandable that the public mania for Sherlock Holmes might have led Doyle to fear that his label as the creator of the Great Detective would somehow prevent his entrance into the Valhalla of literature. In fact, however, since Doyle's great aim was to be the Sir Walter Scott of his generation, he was handicapped from the beginning because historical fiction had by that time gone out of fashion. Even if fine novels like *The White Company* were as great as *Ivanhoe* and sold well, the problem was that the work of Scott himself was already fading in popularity by the latter part of the nineteenth century. More important perhaps, while Doyle was equally adept at his mystery and his historical-adventure fiction, his work does not reach the dimensions of his greatest contemporaries. He cannot, for example, match the brilliance of George Meredith, nor the broad vision of Thomas Hardy or Joseph Conrad. At the same time, in his own field he is unmatched, and he has the distinction of having created in Sherlock Holmes a figure so real that generations of readers have written to him at 221B Baker Street to enlist his help.

Doyle himself was an interesting combination of his own Holmes and Watson. "I have often been asked," he remarks in his memoirs, "whether I had myself the qualities which I depicted [in Holmes], or whether I was merely the Watson that I look."[19] He was indeed to all appearances like the forthright and chivalrous Watson. In his biography of Doyle, Hesketh Pearson describes him "in the first flush of his fame: a simple, reserved, proud, friendly, outspoken, warm-hearted, hot-headed big boy of a man."[20] The image of Sherlock Holmes—tall and lean, with sharp, piercing eyes and a hawklike nose—is so stamped upon the reader's consciousness that persons meeting Doyle himself sometimes failed to realize that Holmes's keen brain inhabited that Watson-like body. Yet Doyle did occasionally take on the real-life role of his own Sherlock Holmes, following up clues and analyzing evidence in the cause of justice.

Perhaps the most interesting of these cases was that of George Edalji, in which Doyle not only achieved a pardon for the victim but tracked down the real culprit in true Holmesian fashion.[21] The circumstances were these. In the village of Great Wryley, twenty miles from Birmingham, there had been an epidemic of animal maiming from February to August of 1903. Horses, cows, sheep, and ponies had been found with their bellies ripped by a sharp-bladed instrument. At the same time, the police had received anonymous letters which gloated over the crimes and at the same time accused George Edalji of being the guilty man.

George was the son of the Reverend Shapurji Edalji, a Parsee from India, who had become a clergyman in the Church of England, had married an English lady, and had been vicar of Great Wryley for thirty years. George, now twenty-seven, was a solicitor in Birmingham. As a boy, he had been a brilliant student, receiving many honors, and was now a highly respected attorney. Slight, frail, and reticent, he was an unlikely suspect at best, but the chief constable of Staffordshire, George Anson, was only too ready to find him guilty. A stolid man who admittedly loathed "black" people, he had nourished an unreasoning prejudice against George Edalji for many years. During a period from 1892 to 1895, the village had been inundated with anonymous letters, many of which constituted attacks on the Edalji family. The chief constable took it into his head that they were the work of George, then a schoolboy, and remained blind to any evidence to the contrary, of which there was plenty.

Thus, on August 18, 1903, when yet another animal had been found maimed in a field, Anson decided to move against George Edalji. Accompanied by several police officers, he went to the Edalji home after George had departed for the city and asked to examine his clothing. He found mud on some boots and trousers and declared that a coat was damp and contained horsehairs, although Edalji's parents and sister hotly denied the slightest appearance of such hairs. Anson then took the coat and vest, which in transit to the police station were wrapped in a bundle together with a strip of hide from the pony that had died that morning. If no horsehairs were present before, they were certainly present now when the coat was again examined. George Edalji was arrested that day.

When Doyle delved into the reports of the case and the transcript of the trial, he was appalled at the clear indications that the police had either tampered with the evidence or at best proceeded with what could only be described as calculated incompetence. In addition to the suspect hairs on the coat, they called into evidencee two very small spots of "blood" on the cuff of the coat, which might, in fact, have been gravy, and which would scarcely be significant in the presence of such copious blood as must have covered the perpetrator of the maimings. They entered as evidence the mud on the clothing, without making the distinction the author of Sherlock Holmes pointed out between the dark mud of the road where Edalji had walked and the yellowish-red soil of the fields. As for footprints, they had trampled all over the scene of the crime and then later taken one of Edalji's shoes, pressed it down near the scene of the attack on the pony, and claimed it matched other prints, relying on measurements done with "bits of stick" and a straw, and failing to take casts of any of the footprints.

The time element presented another startling condemnation of the police case. At first, the time of the crime was set between eight and nine-thirty of the previous evening, when George was known to have walked into the village. It then appeared that George had for many years slept in the bedroom with his father, with the door locked (perhaps a form of Edwardian birth control?) and that the father, a light sleeper, would have heard him had he left the room. Furthermore, a veterinarian testified that the pony could not have been injured earlier than 2:30 A.M. and probably later, upon which the time of the crime was duly changed to early morning. The fact that another maiming occurred while George was awaiting trial was totally ignored.

Despite the flimsy evidence, and amid a good deal of public protest at the time of the trial, George Edalji was convicted and sentenced to seven years of penal servitude. Then a curious thing happened: when he had served three years of his sentence, he was quietly released but not pardoned. Certainly his release was a tacit admission that, in Tennysonian phrase, "someone had blundered," but without a pardon Edalji remained a convicted felon and could not practice law. It was at this point that Doyle took up the cause. After studying all of the available records, Doyle arranged to meet George Edalji in person. Arriving a bit late, he found the young man reading a newspaper to pass the time, and was immediately assured of his innocence. Noting that Edalji held the paper close to his eyes and rather sideways, he exclaimed, "You suffer from astigmatic myopia, I perceive!" His study of the eye, which had never brought him a patient, now came into its own, for as he indignantly declared, no one with Edalji's limited vision could possibly have committed the atrocities for which he had been convicted. How could he have roamed the countryside at night, crossing fields and railway lines in the dark, when he was half-blind even in broad daylight?

Soon after his meeting with George Edalji in January, 1907, Doyle began to publish a series of articles in the *Daily Telegraph* on the case, which aroused enormous public concern. At last the Home Office consented to appoint a committee of three unbiased persons to examine the case and to recommend whatever official action should be taken.

Meanwhile, not content with hoping for a pardon for Edalji, Doyle set about to find the real culprit. Beginning with the first group of anonymous letters from the years 1892 to 1895, he determined that they had been written by two persons, one a fairly literate man, and the other a foul-mouthed semiliterate boy. By both handwriting and internal evidence, he confirmed that the letters of 1903, which began to appear at the time of the mutilations, were entirely by Foul Mouth, now a grown man, and that he was undoubtedly the one who committed the crimes. From frequent references in the letters to his hatred for the headmaster of Walsall Grammar School, it was obvious that the boy had been a student there. Doyle then pointed out what no one seemed to have considered—the significance of the seven years between 1895 and 1903 in which the anonymous letters had totally ceased to appear in Great Wryley. When they began again in 1903 they were filled with references to the sea.

Putting these facts together, Doyle was able to identify Foul Mouth as a boy who had been expelled from Walsall at the age of thirteen as an incorrigible. He had a record of violence, including the curious habit of ripping up cushions in railway carriages to expose the horsehair inside, and he had been guilty of crude attempts at forging letters. He was apprenticed to a butcher, thus becoming familiar with instruments for cutting animal meat. In December, 1895, he went to sea, where he remained until early in 1903, at which time he returned to Great Wryley and was living there during the entire time of the mutilations. Giving the man the fictitious name of "Peter

Hudson" (no relation, we trust, to the long-suffering land-lady of Baker Street), Doyle made out a damning case against him. He found a neighbor of "Hudson" who described how "Peter" had shown her a large horse lancet and said, "This is what they kill cattle with." He showed by handwriting that Peter's older brother had collaborated in the letters of 1892–95. Most damning of all, perhaps, was that during the time Doyle was investigating the case against Hudson, he himself began receiving vile and threatening letters which were obviously from the same anonymous source as those in the Great Wryley case. They seethed with hatred of the headmaster of Walsall Grammar School and of "all black and yellow faced Jews," and obsessively repeated that George Edalji had written all of the anonymous letters, including presumably the very ones now being sent to Doyle.

Doyle carefully summarized this evidence for the Home Office committee, using for their eyes only the real name of the culprit. Together with the other evidence of Edalji's innocence, he and the distinguished lawyers who presented the case were confident that the result could only be total exoneration and a handsome compensation to Edalji for his three years of wrongful imprisonment. It was with shock and incredulity that they read the decision of the committee when it was made public in May, 1907. The committee agreed that George Edalji had been wrongly convicted of horse-maiming and recommended his pardon on that offense. However, they believed that Edalji had written the anonymous letters and had therefore to some extent "brought his troubles on himself."

Therefore he would be denied any compensation for his three years in prison.

Enraged by the fatuity of the decision, Doyle desperately battled to pursue the prosecution of Peter Hudson, but officialdom remained immune to all reason and declined to file charges or to admit Edalji's innocence of the letter-writing. Surely, exclaimed Doyle, you cannot believe that Edalji would write threatening letters to *me*, while I was engaged in his defense? No reply. And so the case ended. The larger issue had been won. Edalji's pardon made it possible for him to be readmitted to the bar, warmly supported by the legal profession. And in September, 1907, when Sir Arthur was married to Jean Leckie in an elegant and exclusive ceremony at St. Margaret's, Westminister, the most honored guest was George Edalji.

The qualities of both Holmes and Watson which merged in the character of Arthur Conan Doyle are peculiarly English, setting the stage for the classical school of detective fiction, which has flourished in Great Britain since the first appearance of the Great Detective and his friend. Poe's Auguste Dupin had an air of ennui that Holmes sometimes shared at times of inactivity but which was instantly shed at the trumpet call of a new case. Emile Gaboriau and other practitioners of the French school of the crime novel often depicted a society so depraved that the reader seeks in vain for a sympathetic character, while the French detectives are likely to be more cynical, sly, and tricky than their English counterparts. Sherlock Holmes

displays essentially all of the British middle-class virtues—
the dedication to truth and justice exhibited by Inspector
Bucket and Sergeant Cuff—but with a brilliance and flair
beyond the scope of the earnest plodders. While Holmes
eschews romantic sentimentality, he is as eager as Watson
to see that justice triumphs and the guilty are punished.
Those who come to him for help, from a lowly typist to
a duchess, are treated with equal consideration. Little
wonder that he stirred the hearts of his readers and became a household word from the days of his first appearance in the *Strand Magazine* stories.

The fame of Sherlock Holmes is not confined to those
who have actually read Doyle's stories. Hesketh Pearson
hazards a guess that Holmes is one of that stellar company
whose names have become symbols for some universal
quality: "Any coal-heaver, docker, charwoman, or pub-
lican would recognise what was meant on hearing someone
described a 'reg'lar Romeo' or 'a blasted Shylock' or 'a
blinkin' Robinson Crusoe' or 'a bleedin' Sherlock
Holmes.'"[22] It is regrettable that Doyle himself deprecated
his own splendid achievement, for generations of readers
have found stimulation, solace, and delight in the exploits
of Sherlock and his loyal friend.

Notes

Chapter 1: BEGINNINGS: THE LONDON CONSTABULARY

1. Dorothy L. Sayers, ed., *The Omnibus of Crime* (New York: Harcourt, Brace, 1929), 11.
2. Sources for the history of the British police are Douglas C. Browne, *The Rise of Scotland Yard: A History of the Metropolitan Police* (London: Harrap, 1956), and Patrick Pringle, *Hue and Cry: The Birth of the British Police* (London: Museum Press, 1955).
3. E. F. Bleiler, "Introduction," *Richmond: Scenes in the Life of a Bow Street Runner* (New York: Dover Press, 1976), viii.
4. *Ibid.*, ix–x.
5. *Ibid.*, 87.
6. *Ibid.*, 241.
7. Ian Ousby, *Bloodhounds of Heaven: The Detective in English Fiction from Godwin to Doyle* (Cambridge, Mass.: Harvard University Press, 1976), 46.
8. *Ibid.*, 45.
9. François Eugène Vidocq, *Memoirs of Vidocq: The Principal Agent of the French Police* (Philadelphia: T. B. Peterson, 1859), *passim*.
10. See Ousby, p. 66, for date and authorship of these stories.
11. Waters [pseud.], *Recollections of a Detective Police-Officer* (London: J. & C. Brown, 1856), 36.
12. *Ibid.*, "Preface."

Chapter 2: WILKIE COLLINS AND THE MYSTERY NOVEL

1. Robert Ashley, *Wilkie Collins* (London: Barker, 1951), 105.
2. Wilkie Collins, *Memoirs of the Life of William Collins, Esq., R.A.* (London: Longman, 1848).

3. Wilkie Collins, "Reminiscences of a Story-Teller," *The Universal Review* (May–August 1888).

4. Kenneth Robinson, *Wilkie Collins: A Biography* (c. 1951; rpt. London: Davis-Poynter, 1974), 59–60. This excellent biography is the chief source for information on Collins's life. Dorothy L. Sayers began a life of Collins, but the manuscript covers only the early years of his life (*Wilkie Collins: A Critical and Biographical Study*, ed. E. R. Gregory [Toledo, Ohio: The Friends of the Univ. of Toledo Library, 1977]).

5. Robinson, 102.

6. *The Letters of Charles Dickens*, ed. Walter Dexter (Bloomsbury: Nonesuch Press, 1938). All letters cited are from this edition. Because Dickens made a bonfire at Gads Hill of his friends' correspondence, we have none of Collins's letters to him. Fortunately Dickens's own letters have survived and provide the source for much of what is known of the friendship.

7. John Guille Millais, *The Life and Letters of Sir John Everett Millais* (New York: Frederick Stoker, 1899), vol. I, p. 278.

8. Clyde K. Hyder, "Wilkie Collins and *The Woman in White*," *PMLA*, 54 (March 1939):297–303.

9. Gladys Storey, *Dickens and Daughter* (London: Frederick Muller, 1939), 213–14.

10. Robinson, 124.

11. *Ibid.*, 125.

12. R. C. Lehmann, *Memories of Half a Century* (London: Smith, Elder, 1908), 29.

13. Robinson, 207.

14. Dickens, *Letters*, 19 August 1860.

15. *Ibid.*, 12 July 1866.

16. Nuel Pharr Davis, *The Life of Wilkie Collins* (Urbana: University of Illinois Press, 1956).

17. Dickens also used the circus scenario in *Hard Times*, which came out in the same year as *Hide and Seek*, perhaps indicating a shared pleasure.

18. See Henry J. W. Milley, "Wilkie Collins and *A Tale of Two Cities*," *Modern Language Review*, 34 (1939):525–534.

19. Norman Page, ed., *Wilkie Collins: The Critical Heritage* (London: Routledge and Kegan Paul, 1974), 69, 71.

20. *Ibid.*, 71.

21. Davis, 179.

22. Robert Ashley, "Wilkie Collins and the Detective Story," *Nineteenth-Century Fiction*, 6 (1951):50.
23. Dickens, *Letters*, 13 July 1856.
24. S. M. Ellis, *Wilkie Collins, Le Fanu, and Others* (c. 1931; rpt. London: Constable, 1951), 29–30.
25. This source was first identified by Clyde K. Hyder (see Note 8 above).
26. Wilkie Collins, *The Woman in White* (London: Oxford University Press, 1975), 5. All citations are from this edition.
27. Page, 131, 143.
28. T. S. Eliot, *Selected Essays* (New York: Harcourt, Brace, 1932), 416.
29. Page, 147.
30. Dorothy L. Sayers, "Introduction," *The Omnibus of Crime* (New York: Harcourt, Brace, 1929), 25.
31. Ashley, *Wilkie Collins*, 91–92.
32. Page, 262.

Chapter 3: DICKENS AND DETECTION

1. The principal sources for Dickens's biography are John Forster, *The Life of Charles Dickens* (New York: Scribners, 1905, 2 vols.), and Edgar Johnson, *Charles Dickens: His Tragedy and Triumph* (New York: Simon and Schuster, 1952, 2 vols.).
2. Forster, I, 26–27.
3. References to the Ellen Ternan affair are not found in Forster. See Johnson, II, Ch. 5, *passim*, and other modern biographies.
4. Johnson, II, 882.
5. Philip Collins, *Dickens and Crime* (London: Macmillan, 1962), 274.
6. Keith Hollingsworth notes that Jonas may be based upon the forger and murderer, Thomas Wainewright, whose case interested Dickens (*The Newgate Novel* [Detroit: Wayne State University Press, 1963], 183–185.)
7. Charles Dickens, "Reprinted Pieces," in *The Works of Charles Dickens* (London: Chapman and Hall, 1899), XXXIV, 140.
8. *Ibid.*
9. *Ibid.*, 142–43.
10. *Ibid.*, 161.
11. *Ibid.*, 177–78.
12. Philip Collins, 206.

13. See Leon Garfield, *"The Mystery of Edwin Drood" by Charles Dickens: Concluded by Leon Garfield* (New York: Pantheon Books, 1980).
14. Forster, II, 452.
15. *Ibid.*
16. See the excellent analysis of Forster's character in Hesketh Pearson, *Dickens: His Character, Comedy, and Career* (New York: Harper's, 1949), Ch. 5.
17. Rpt. in W. Robertson Nicoll, *The Problem of "Edwin Drood": A Study in the Methods of Dickens* (London: Hodder and Stoughton, n.d. [1912]), 32–33.
18. *Ibid.*, 31–32; 34; 42–43.
19. Margaret Cardwell, "Introduction," *The Mystery of Edwin Drood* by Charles Dickens (Oxford: Clarendon Press, 1972), xxvii.
20. Felix Aylmer, *The Drood Case* (New York: Barnes and Noble, 1964), 205.
21. Quoted in Nicoll, 55.
22. See Richard A. Proctor, *Watched by the Dead: A Loving Study of Dicken's Half-Told Tale* (London: W. H. Allen, 1887).
23. Quoted in J. Cuming Walters, *The Complete "Mystery of Edwin Drood" by Charles Dickens: The History, Continuations, and Solutions* (London: Chapman and Hall, 1912), 241.
24. *Ibid.*
25. Nicoll, 159–164.
26. Richard M. Baker, *The Drood Murder Case: Five Studies in Dickens's "Edwin Drood"* (Berkeley: University of California Press), 1–41.
27. Rpt. in Bill Blackbeard, *Sherlock Holmes in America* (New York: Harry N. Abrams, 1981).
28. *Ibid.*, 222.
29. Lillian de la Torre, "John Dickson Carr's Solution to *The Mystery of Edwin Drood*," *The Armchair Detective* 14 (1981):291–294.
30. I am indebted to my colleague, Professor Arthur Axelrad, for this intriguing theory.

Chapter 4: JOSEPH SHERIDAN LE FANU: HORROR AND SUSPENSE

1. Sources for Le Fanu biography are S. M. Ellis, *Wilkie Collins, Le Fanu, and Others* (London: Constable, 1951; c. 1931); Nelson Browne, *Sheridan Le Fanu* (London: Arthur Barker, 1951); and W. J. McCormack, *Sheridan Le Fanu and Victorian Ireland* (Oxford: Clarendon Press, 1980).

2. McCormack corrects the date 1844 given by Ellis and Browne; 114.

3. *Ibid.*, 128.

4. Browne, 31.

5. M. R. James, ed., "Prologue," *Madam Crowl's Ghost and Other Tales of Mystery* by Joseph Sheridan Le Fanu (London: G. Bell, 1923).

6. Elizabeth Bowen, "Introduction," *The House by the Churchyard* by Joseph Sheridan Le Fanu (New York: Stein and Day, 1968), vii, x.

7. McCormack, 140.

8. Ellis, 161.

9. McCormack, 223.

10. Dorothy L. Sayers, ed., *The Omnibus of Crime* (New York: Harcourt, Brace, 1929), 24.

Chapter 5: SOME MINOR VOICES

1. Robert Lee Wolff, *Sensational Victorian: The Life and Fiction of Mary Elizabeth Braddon* (New York: Garland, 1979).

2. *Ibid.*, 35.

3. *Ibid.*, 45.

4. W. B. Maxwell, *Time Gathered: Autobiography* (New York: Appleton-Century, 1938), 281.

5. Wolff, 154–55.

6. *Ibid.*, 2.

7. *Ibid.*, 8, 11, 12.

8. *Ibid.*, 250.

9. Maxwell, 280–81.

10. James Payn, *Some Literary Recollections* (New York: Harper, 1884), 14.

11. *Ibid.*, 56.

12. *Ibid.*, 176.

13. Jacques Barzun and Wendell Hertig Taylor, *A Catalogue of Crime* (New York: Harper and Row, 1971), 337.

14. Quoted in John Dickson Carr, *The Life of Sir Arthur Conan Doyle* (New York: Harper, 1949), 47.

15. *Ibid.*, 60.

16. Hesketh Pearson, *Conan Doyle: His Life and Art* (London: Methuen, 1943), 78.

17. Leslie Stephen, "Introduction," *The Backwater of Life: or Essays of A Literary Veteran* by James Payn (London: Smith, Elder, 1899), xxxii–xxxiii.

18. Payn, *Some Literary Recollections,* 182.
19. Kathleen Woodward, "Anna Katharine Green," *The Bookman* (Oct. 1929): 168.
20. See the *Dictionary of American Biography.*
21. Michele Slung, "Introduction," *The Leavenworth Case* by Anna Katharine Green (New York: Dover, 1981), iv.

Chapter 6: ARTHUR CONAN DOYLE AND THE GREAT DETECTIVE

1. Arthur Conan Doyle, *Memories and Adventures,* 2nd ed. (London: John Murray, 1930), 15.
2. *Ibid.,* 40.
3. *Science* 4 (March 1983): 6.
4. Doyle, 89.
5. *Ibid.*
6. Hesketh Pearson, *Conan Doyle: His Life and Art* (London: Methuen, 1943), 75.
7. John Dickson Carr, *The Life of Sir Arthur Conan Doyle* (New York: Harper, 1949), 41.
8. Doyle, 93.
9. *Ibid.,* 89.
10. *Ibid.,* 33.
11. *Ibid.,* 90.
12. Carr, 55–56.
13. *Ibid.,* 57.
14. *Ibid.,* 58.
15. *Ibid.,* 60.
16. Doyle, 113.
17. Carr, 66.
18. Doyle, 96.
19. *Ibid.,* 118.
20. Pearson, 104.
21. There are various reports of the Edalji case in print; I have chiefly followed here the excellent account in John Dickson Carr, Chapter 15.
22. Pearson, 86.

Suggested Reading

MARY ELIZABETH BRADDON

Lady Audley's Secret (1862)
Aurora Floyd (1863)
Eleanor's Victory (1863)
Henry Dunbar (1864)
Birds of Prey (1867)
Charlotte's Inheritance (1868)
A Strange World (1875)
An Open Verdict (1878)

WILKIE COLLINS

Basil: a Story of Modern Life (1852)
Hide and Seek, or The Mystery of Mary Grice (1854)
After Dark (Short stories) *(1856)*
The Dead Secret (1857)
The Queen of Hearts (Short stories) *(1859)*
The Woman in White (1860)
No Name (1862)
Armadale (1866)
The Moonstone (1868)
Man and Wife (1870)
The Law and the Lady (1875)
The Haunted Hotel and *My Lady's Money (1879)*
Little Novels (Short stories) *(1887)*

CHARLES DICKENS

The Mystery of Edwin Drood (1870) is Dickens's only mystery novel. Other novels containing partial mystery plots and/or detective figures include *Barnaby Rudge (1841)*, *Martin Chuzzlewit (1844)*, and *Bleak House (1852)*.

ARTHUR CONAN DOYLE

A Study in Scarlet (1887)
The Sign of Four (1890)
The Firm of Girdlestone (1890)
The Adventures of Sherlock Holmes (1892)
The Memoirs of Sherlock Holmes (1894)
The Hound of the Baskervilles (1902)
The Return of Sherlock Holmes (1905)
The Valley of Fear (1915)
His Last Bow (1917)
The Case-Book of Sherlock Holmes (1927)

ANNA KATHARINE GREEN

The Leavenworth Case: A Lawyer's Story (1878)
A Strange Disappearance (1880)
The Sword of Damocles: A Story of New York (1881)
XYZ (1883)
Hand and Ring (1883)
Behind Closed Doors (1883)
That Affair Next Door (1888)
Lost Man's Lane: A Second Episode in the Life of Amelia Butterworth (1898)
The Circular Study (1900)
The Filigree Ball (1903)
The Golden Slipper and Other Problems for Violet Strange (1915)

JOSEPH SHERIDAN LE FANU

The House by the Churchyard (1863)
Wylder's Hand (1864)
Uncle Silas (1864)
Guy Deverell (1865)
Checkmate (1871)
The Rose and the Key (1871)

JAMES PAYN

Lost Sir Massingberd (1864)
Like Father, Like Son (1871)
By Proxy (1878)
A Confidential Agent (1880)
The Mystery of Mirbridge (1888)

Bibliography

Ashley, Robert P. *Wilkie Collins*. London: Arthur Barker, 1952.
————. "Wilkie Collins and the Detective Story." *Nineteenth-Century Fiction* 6 (1951): 47–60.
Aylmer, Felix. *The Drood Case*. New York: Barnes and Noble, 1965.
Baker, Richard M. *The Drood Murder Case: Five Studies in Dickens's "Edwin Drood."* Berkeley: University of California Press, 1951.
Barnes, Melvyn. *Best Detective Fiction: A Guide from Godwin to the Present*. London: Clive Bingley and Hamden, Conn: Linnet Books, 1975.
Barzun, Jacques and Wendell Hertig Taylor. *A Catalogue of Crime*. New York: Harper and Row, 1971.
Beetz, Kirk H. *Wilkie Collins: An Annotated Bibliography, 1889–1976*. Metuchen, New Jersey: Scarecrow Press, 1978.
Begnal, Michael H. *Joseph Sheridan Le Fanu*. Lewisburg: Bucknell University Press, 1971.
Blackbeard, Bill. *Sherlock Holmes in America*. New York: Harry N. Abrams, 1981.
Bleiler, E. F. "Introduction," *Richmond: Scenes in the Life of a Bow Street Runner*. New York: Dover, 1976.
Bowen, Elizabeth. "Introduction," *The House by the Churchyard* by J. Sheridan Le Fanu. New York: Stein and Day, 1968.
Brown, Ivor. *Conan Doyle: A Biography of the Creator of Sherlock Holmes*. London: Hamish Hamilton, 1972.
Browne, Douglas G. *The Rise of Scotland Yard: A History of the Metropolitan Police*. London: Harrap, 1956.
Browne, Nelson. *Sheridan Le Fanu*. London: Arthur Barker, 1951.
Caine, Hall. *My Story*. New York: Appleton, 1909.
Cardwell, Margaret, ed. *The Mystery of Edwin Drood* by Charles Dickens. Oxford: Clarendon Press, 1972.

Carr, John Dickson. *The Life of Sir Arthur Conan Doyle*. New York: Harper, 1949.

Chandler, Frank W. *The Literature of Roguery*. New York: Burt Franklin, 1958. 2 vols.

Collins, Philip. *Dickens and Crime*. London: Macmillan, 1962.

Collins, W. Wilkie. *Memoirs of the Life of William Collins, Esq., R.A.*, . . . London: Longman, Brown, Green, and Longmans, 1848.

———. "Reminiscences of a Story-Teller," *The Universal Review* (May—August): 1888.

Dakin, D. Martin. *A Sherlock Holmes Commentary*. New York: Drake, 1972.

Davis, Nuel Pharr. *The Life of Wilkie Collins*. Urbana: University of Illinois Press, 1956.

De la Torre, Lillian. "John Dickson Carr's Solution to *The Mystery of Edwin Drood*." *The Armchair Detective* 14 (1981), 291–294.

Dickens, Charles. *The Letters of Charles Dickens*, ed. Walter Dexter. Bloomsbury: The Nonesuch Press, 1938, 3 vols.

Doyle, Arthur Conan. *Memories and Adventures*, 2nd ed. London: John Murray, 1930.

Eliot, T. S. *Selected Essays*. New York: Harcourt, Brace, 1932.

Ellis, S. M. *Wilkie Collins, Le Fanu, and Others*. London: Constable, 1951 [c. 1931].

Elwin, Malcolm. *Victorian Wallflowers*. C. 1934; rpt. New York: Kennikat Press, 1966.

Forster, John. *The Life of Charles Dickens*. New York: Scribner's, 1905. 2 vols.

Garfield, Leon. *"The Mystery of Edwin Drood" by Charles Dickens, Concluded by Leon Garfield*. New York: Pantheon Books, 1980.

Glover, Dorothy and Graham Greene. *Victorian Detective Fiction: A Catalogue of the Collection made by Dorothy Glover and Graham Green*. . . . London: Bodley Head, 1966.

Hagen, Ordean A. *Who Done It: A Guide to Detective, Mystery, and Suspense Fiction*. New York: Bowker, 1969.

Haycraft, Howard. *Murder for Pleasure: The Life and Times of the Detective Story*. New York: Appleton-Century, 1941; 1968.

Hollingsworth, Keith. *The Newgate Novel, 1830–1847: Bulwer, Ainsworth, Dickens, and Thackeray*. Detroit: Wayne State University Press, 1963.

Hyder, Clyde K. "Wilkie Collins and *The Woman in White*." *PMLA*, 54 (1939), 297–303.

James, M. R., ed. *Madam Crowl's Ghost and Other Tales of Mystery* by Joseph Sheridan Le Fanu. London: G. Bell, 1923.

Johnson, Edgar. *Charles Dickens: His Tragedy and Triumph*. New York: Simon and Schuster, 1952. 2 vols.

Lehmann, R. C. *Memories of Half a Century: A Record of Friendships*. London: Smith, Elder, 1908.

Maxwell, W. B. *Time Gathered: Autobiography*. New York: Appleton-Century, 1938.

McCormack, W. J. *Sheridan Le Fanu and Victorian Ireland*. Oxford: Clarendon Press, 1980.

Millais, John Guille. *The Life and Letters of Sir John Everett Millais*. New York: Frederick Stoker, 1899, 2 vols.

Milley, Henry J. W. "Wilkie Collins and *A Tale of Two Cities*." *Modern Language Review* 34 (1939): 525–534.

Murch, A. E. *The Development of the Detective Novel*. Port Washington, New York: Kennikat Press, 1968.

Nicoll, W. Robertson. *The Problem of "Edwin Drood": A Study in the Methods of Dickens*. London: Hodder and Stoughton, n.d. [1912].

Ousby, Ian. *Bloodhounds of Heaven: The Detective in English Fiction from Godwin to Doyle*. Cambridge: Mass: Harvard University Press, 1976.

Page, Norman, ed. *Wilkie Collins: The Critical Heritage*. London: Routledge and Kegan Paul, 1974.

Payn, James. *Some Literary Recollections*. New York: Harper, 1884.

Pearsall, Ronald. *Conan Doyle: A Biographical Solution*. London: Weidenfeld and Nicolson, 1977.

Pearson, Hesketh. *Conan Doyle: His Life and Art*. London: Methuen, 1943.

———. *Dickens: His Character, Comedy, and Career*. New York: Harper, 1949.

Phillips, Walter C. *Dickens, Reade, and Collins: Sensation Novelists*. New York: Columbia University Press, 1919.

Pringle, Patrick. *Hue and Cry: The Birth of the British Police*. London: Museum Press, 1955.

Proctor, Richard A. *Watched by the Dead: A Loving Study of Dickens's Half-Told Tale*. London: W. H. Allen, 1887.

Quayle, Eric S. *The Collector's Book of Detective Fiction*. London: Studio Vista, 1972.

Richmond [pseud.]. *Richmond: Scenes in the Life of a Bow Street Runner*, ed. E. F. Bleiler. New York: Dover, 1976.

Robinson, Kenneth. *Wilkie Collins: A Biography*. London: Bodley Head, 1951.

Sadleir, Michael. *Excursions in Victorian Bibliography*. London: Chauncey and Cox, 1922.

Sayers, Dorothy L., ed. *The Omnibus of Crime*. New York: Harcourt, Brace, 1929.

————. *Wilkie Collins: A Critical and Biographical Study*, ed. from the Manuscript by E. R. Gregory. Toledo, Ohio: The Friends of the University of Toledo Library, 1977. [Unfinished biography.]

Smith, Harry B. "Sherlock Holmes Solves the Mystery of Edwin Drood." *Munsey Magazine*, 1924: rpt. Bill Blackbeard, *Sherlock Holmes in America*. New York: Harry N. Abrams, 1981.

Stephen, Leslie. "Introduction," *the Backwater of Life: or Essays of a Literary Veteran* by James Payn. London: Smith, Elder, 1899.

Storey, Gladys. *Dickens and Daughter*. London: Frederick Muller, 1939.

Thomson, H. Douglas. *Masters of Mystery: A Study of the Detective Story*. London: Collins, 1931.

Vidocq, François Eugène. *Memoirs of Vidocq: The Principal Agent of the French Police, Written by Himself*. Philadelphia: T. B. Peterson, 1859.

Walters, J. Cuming. *The Complete Mystery of Edwin Drood by Charles Dickens: The History, Continuations, and Solutions, 1870–1912*. London: Chapman and Hall, 1912.

Waters [pseud.]. *Recollections of a Detective Police-Officer*. London: J. and C. Brown, 1856.

Watson, Colin. *Snobbery with Violence: Crime Stories and their Audience*. London: Eyre and Spottiswoode, 1971.

Wolff, Robert Lee. *Sensational Victorian: The Life and Fiction of Mary Elizabeth Braddon*. New York: Garland, 1979.

Woodward, Kathleen. "Anna Katharine Green," *The Bookman* (October, 1929): 168.

Index

231